Praise for *Saving Face*

"In *Saving Face*, Maya shows us what we can learn from other cultures with real and practical examples that will help leaders and teams become even more effective."
—**Jim Moore, former Chief Learning Officer, Sun Microsystems and Nortel**

"The need to save face is a fundamental part of doing business. It is hard work, but the payoff is immense. A must-read and a must-add to any professional portfolio."
—**CB Bowman, MBA, CMC, BCC, MCEC, CEO, Association of Corporate Executive Coaches and MEECO Leadership Institute**

"*Saving Face* is a highly enjoyable read that will help us all up our skills in this critical enabler of trusting, meaningful, and successful relationships."
—**Darlene Solomon, PhD, Chief Technology Officer, Agilent Technologies**

"Maya is truly an expert on global agility. She knows that this topic is like a brilliant crystal, with many different facets to be examined and explored. I highly recommend this book!"
—**Patty McKay, Global Vice President, Talent Development, 3D Systems**

"Great conflicts—even entire wars—have begun due to misunderstandings around saving face. One of the world's great intercultural communication experts, Maya Hu-Chan, beautifully teaches us how saving face operates in our day-to-day lives and how to better use it to build trusting relationships in business and beyond."
—**Brian O. Underhill, PhD, PCC, founder and CEO, CoachSource, LLC, and author of *Executive Coaching for Results***

"With candor, humor, and plenty of real-life examples, Maya shows how to leverage the critical competency of saving face to build business relationships. If you want to grow your global leadership and business presence, you need to read this book!"
—**Dr. Ann Bowers-Evangelista, President, Llumos, LLC, and executive consultant and coach based in Japan**

"Read *Saving Face* if you are interested in having a positive impact on all those with whom you interact and making your contribution to a world where polite and caring discourse prevails."
—**Beth Schumaker, Senior Partner, BrightStar Leadership Consulting**

"Maya has leveraged her experiences in working in dozens of countries across the globe to examine a topic common to all cultures—saving face. I would especially recommend this book to people who deal with others in a multicultural environment."

—Bill Hawkins, contributing author of five books, including *What Got You Here Won't Get You There in Sales*

"A must-read for every leader, especially when working with multicultural teams."

—Brigitta Wurnig, international coach and author of *Auf dem Weg* (*On the Way*)

"Maya has put her finger on a very relevant and timely issue in the multicultural world we live and work in. Loaded with practical ideas and examples, derived from her vast national and international experience in executive development, her work offers an important contribution to all those interested in furthering their ability to communicate honestly and directly while preserving dignity and building trust."

—Carlos E. Marin, President, C. E. Marin & Associates

"Finally, a book that addresses an often-ignored aspect of business success. In this well-written work, a plethora of anecdotes perfectly illustrates the challenges and solutions for the multifaceted issue of face. *Saving Face* is an absolute 'must' for making this abstract topic an essential part of your business relationship tool kit."

—Diana K. Rowland, bestselling author and President, IntXel

"This is a must-read guide for global leaders who want to create impact through positive relationships."

—Eun Y. Kim, PhD, author of *The Yin and Yang of American Culture*

"Maya Hu-Chan is truly a master of helping successful people improve. The wisdom found in this book can help any leader, from the one who is already considered excellent with strong interpersonal skills to the leader who appears to be clueless in interactions with others."

—Dr. Frank Wagner, Master Coach and cofounder of Stakeholder-Centered Coaching

"*Saving Face* engagingly illuminates an extraordinarily important, yet often misunderstood, concept and lays out a clear path forward for us all."

—Gregg Ward, MCES, bestselling, award-winning author of *The Respectful Leader*

"*Saving Face* is a must-read for all those who need to enhance their emotional intelligence, cultural agility, and ability to recognize and recover from communication pitfalls—which, as you might guess, is just about all of us."

—Joel Garfinkle, author of *Getting Ahead*

"*Saving Face* describes a globally relevant concept through subtle and nuanced cultural lenses, also providing strategies on how to avoid behaviors that will cause someone to lose face. It is a must-read!"

—Judith Eberl, Managing Director, JuPantaRhei GmbH, Switzerland; former Head of Training and Development, EFG Bank SA; and former Head of International Education, Assicurazioni Generali S.p.A.

"*Saving Face* is a powerful book that unpacks the concept of saving face with practical examples of how to develop the deep and authentic interactions necessary for successful business partnerships. A must-read for any leader or team member whether working locally or globally."

—Judith H. Katz, EdD, Executive Vice President, The Kaleel Jamison Consulting Group, Inc., and coauthor with Fred Miller of *Safe Enough to Soar*

"In *Saving Face*, Maya Hu-Chan guides us to step into our truth in a way that transforms ourselves and others with grace, compassion, and honesty—which brings us closer to a universe that is more connected and able to understand rather than flee or fight."

—Louis Carter, CEO, Best Practice Institute, and author of eleven management/leadership books, including the bestselling *In Great Company*

"Drawing on her extraordinary international experience, Maya Hu-Chan transforms the way we think and feel about life's greatest challenges and opportunities with a book that defines saving face like no other. A must-read!"

—Mark C. Thompson, *New York Times* bestselling author and "World's #1 Executive Coach"

"Maya Hu-Chan has set up an outstanding compendium for global leaders. I love her definition of face as social currency in intercultural interaction. This book should be a standard for intercultural training."
—**Matthias Brose, Vice President, Schaeffler AG**

"With Maya Hu-Chan's extensive executive coaching and cross-cultural expertise, she provides valuable and refreshing new insights on how to effectively show respect and build trust with others, which is critical for high performing teams and lasting relationships in the workplace. Everyone needs to read this book!"
—**Nancy E. Parsons, CEO and President, CDR Assessment Group, Inc.**

"I can think of no better person to write a book on saving face than Maya Hu-Chan. Her use of face as a form of social currency is enlightening and practical. This book is a must-read for anyone who wants to understand the fundamental cultural values and behaviors that are hidden until exposed in depth here."
—**Neal R. Goodman, PhD, President, Global Dynamics, and Professor Emeritus, Saint Peter's University**

"As a Scotsman living in Asia for over thirty years, I find Maya Hu-Chan's book an essential guide to all those working outside their own culture and a breath of fresh air for avoiding faux pas and ensuring you save face. Every CEO should give each team member a copy of this book."
—**Robin Speculand, strategy implementation/digital specialist and bestselling author of *Excellence in Execution***

"In *Saving Face*, Maya Hu-Chan brings to light how empathy, trust, and respect are connected to the concepts of saving face and how they are foundational for positive human interactions. A must-read for all."
—**Rosa Grunhaus Belzer, PhD, PCC, Coaching Talent Leader, Western North America, Center for Creative Leadership**

"Maya Hu-Chan is an engaging and authentic expert in global business. In *Saving Face*, she applies her deep knowledge from coaching and consulting to multinational corporations and executives around the world. You don't want to miss it!"
—**Susan Diamond, Vice President and Chief Learning Officer, Women Presidents' Organization**

To Denize —
Thank you for being a
good friend and an
inspiration! — Maya

SAVING FACE

CONNECT,
BREAK DOWN BARRIERS,
AND BUILD TRUST

SAVING FACE

How to Preserve Dignity and Build Trust

SAVING FACE

How to Preserve Dignity
and Build Trust

MAYA HU-CHAN

BK

Berrett–Koehler Publishers, Inc.

Berrett-Koehler Publishers, Inc.
1333 Broadway, Suite 1000, Oakland, CA 94612-1921
Tel: (510) 817-2277   Fax: (510) 817-2278
www.bkconnection.com

ORDERING INFORMATION
Quantity sales. Special discounts are available on quantity purchases by corporations, associations, and others. For details, contact the "Special Sales Department" at the Berrett-Koehler address above.
Individual sales. Berrett-Koehler publications are available through most bookstores. They can also be ordered directly from Berrett-Koehler: Tel: (800) 929-2929; Fax: (802) 864-7626; www.bkconnection.com.
Orders for college textbook / course adoption use. Please contact Berrett-Koehler: Tel: (800) 929-2929; Fax: (802) 864-7626.

Distributed to the U.S. trade and internationally by Penguin Random House Publisher Services.

Berrett-Koehler and the BK logo are registered trademarks of Berrett-Koehler Publishers, Inc.

Printed in the United States of America

Berrett-Koehler books are printed on long-lasting acid-free paper. When it is available, we choose paper that has been manufactured by environmentally responsible processes. These may include using trees grown in sustainable forests, incorporating recycled paper, minimizing chlorine in bleaching, or recycling the energy produced at the paper mill.

Library of Congress Cataloging-in-Publication Data

Names: Hu-Chan, Maya, author.
Title: Saving face : how to preserve dignity and build trust / Maya Hu-Chan.
Description: First edition. | Oakland, CA : Berrett-Koehler Publishers, [2020] | Includes bibliographical references and index.
Identifiers: LCCN 2019054230 | ISBN 9781523088607 (paperback) | ISBN 9781523088614 (pdf) | ISBN 9781523088621 (epub)
Subjects: LCSH: Diversity in the workplace. | Dignity. | Intercultural communication.
Classification: LCC HF5549.5.M5 H79 2020 | DDC 650.1/3—dc23
LC record available at https://lccn.loc.gov/2019054230

First Edition
29 28 27 26 25 24 23 22 21 20   10 9 8 7 6 5 4 3 2 1

Book producer: Wilsted & Taylor Publishing Services
Copyediting: Nancy Evans | Text design: Michael Starkman
Cover design: Adam Johnson

FOR TWO SETS OF PARENTS

Thank you to my parents
for making possible all that I have

Thank you to my in-laws
for making possible all that I am

CONTENTS

In *Saving Face: How to Preserve Dignity and Build Trust*, author, speaker, and executive coach Maya Hu-Chan brings us her unique take on "face." I've known and worked with Maya for more than thirty years and I love this book because it reminds me of a story that one of my great friends and coaching clients, Dr. Jim Yong Kim (former president of the World Bank), has shared with me about what he learned from the great leader Alan Mulally, former CEO of Boeing and Ford.

Dr. Kim said that the greatest thing that he learned from Alan is the idea that as a leader your face is no longer your own. What Alan meant by this, says Dr. Kim, is that, when you show up as a leader, if your face looks angry or upset, people will respond in kind. So, as a leader, you must do your best to be as positive and upbeat, and as sincere and authentic in your facial expressions as you can be.

In her book *Saving Face*, Maya explores this concept of "saving face" more deeply as it relates to cultures around the globe. For instance, have you ever considered saving face as a form of social currency? Beyond monetary currency, it is a form of currency that impacts our status and reputation among all of our many communities, including business, family, and politics.

This is just one of the many interesting ideas that Maya describes in detail while offering suggestions for how we can best manage "face" to connect with people and to create and maintain relationships.

Most critical is Maya's BUILD model, which she offers as the key to saving face when working with people around the globe. BUILD—which stands for benevolence, understanding, interacting, learning, and delivery—represents the five building blocks crucial to the development of great business relationships. It's Maya's gift to us, and in studying and engaging in the use of this essential tool and reading and studying this exceptional book, we can learn to save, honor, and avoid losing face, and thus be the most positive influence in the world that we can be.

Life is good.

MARSHALL GOLDSMITH

The time is right for *Saving Face*. Beyond its origins in China, "saving face" is a universal concept that enables one to connect with people, break down barriers, and build trust and long-term relationships. The concept of saving face permeates all levels of social and business interactions. When the term "It's not about the money" is used, the real issue is often about "face."

On the leadership front, managers, entrepreneurs, and even individual contributors must adapt to increasingly diverse clientele, workforces, and business partners. They need to attract, retain, and motivate teams and employees across distances, time zones, and cultural differences. They must move in many circles, think in many styles, and run their businesses as global citizens.

From a personal standpoint, the concept of saving face is of universal importance. Being able to relate to others, find commonalities, and work toward a common goal are all wrapped up in how each person understands and protects the face of others. No other motivator, including monetary compensation, can truly lead to optimal success in any group setting without considering face, and this book will highlight how that is so.

More than ever, leaders must win the trust and respect of their counterparts. Building authentic and lasting human relations may be the most important calling for leaders in this century.

The ability for people to save and build face is the social currency of our time. It is even more crucially important in today's era of social media, where it is so easy to slight someone without the normal check and balance of having to actually confront them face-to-face with your slight. As the workplace grows in complexity, *Saving Face* will provide priceless guidance and lessons for leaders in the new economic era.

Why is face so important? Face represents one's self-esteem, reputation, status, and dignity. Face is social currency. The more "face" you have, the easier and faster you can get things done. The desire to save face is human nature across cultures, generations, genders, and other human differences.

Why is "losing face" such a bad thing? It provokes shame, fear, guilt, vulnerability, and a wide range of negative emotions. You can cause someone to lose face by giving negative feedback in public, challenging or disagreeing with someone, failing to acknowledge the hierarchy, or engaging in micro-inequity behaviors such as giving subtle insults, ignoring or interrupting someone, making insensitive jokes, and more.

This book explains how we can *honor* face to connect with people and create positive first impressions, how we can inadvertently cause others to *lose* face in business or social situations, and, most important, how we can effectively *save* face to avoid negative consequences.

Saving face means *preserving dignity* for all parties involved in order to reach a positive outcome. It requires that we put ourselves in another person's shoes, understand their frame of reference, take thoughtful actions to navigate potentially harmful situations, and build real trust and long-term relationships in life and business.

Saving face is far more than highlighting the importance of not embarrassing someone. It is also about developing an understanding of the background and motivations of others to discover the unique facets of face that each of us possesses. Without such an understanding, even the most well-intentioned individuals risk causing others to lose face without even knowing it. *Saving Face* provides the tools for individuals and managers to help head off these risks.

The *authentic* act of saving face requires a positive intention and understanding others' frame of reference without judgment. Without positive intention and acceptance, the act of saving face can be perceived as manipulative, superficial, or phony.

In this book, saving face is explained through both illustrative anecdotes and practical tools, such as the AAA model (Aware → Acquire → Adapt) and the BUILD model (Benevolence/Accountability, Understanding, Interacting, Learning, Delivery).

Saving Face is one of the first business books in a global leadership and cross-cultural context to explore the concept of face, the powerful cultural value that reflects one's status in business, family life, and society. Increasingly, more business leaders will need to adapt new mindsets and behaviors to connect effectively with people and successfully navigate the volatile global business landscape.

But even beyond the business aspect of saving face, my hope is that this book will serve as a catalyst for all forms of communications, from those that occur between multinational corporations down to individual interactions of friends and neighbors. While the primary audiences for this book are business leaders, managers, entrepreneurs, and professionals whose work requires them to interact and engage with people of diverse backgrounds to get things done, I also seek in this book to benefit any individual who wants to improve how they relate to others—how teachers relate to their students, how parents communicate with their children, and

in many other social contexts. Those who take the time to
understand the importance of saving face realize that it cov-
ers nearly every aspect of social discourse, and its impact is
universal.

Saving Face shows leaders how to build "face" and forge
stronger, more authentic partnerships with clients and colleagues across cultural, generational, gender, and other human differences. Because business grows more diverse by
the day, this book will appeal to corporate leaders seeking a
wealth of real-life lessons and valuable advice on putting face
into action and guiding global, multicultural teams.

Honoring Face, Losing Face, and Saving Face

HEN IT CAME to writing this book, I asked myself one question: Of the thousands of executives and senior managers I've coached over the years, what was the one concern they would bring up time and time again?

I didn't have to mull over my answer very long. It was all about face. To be sure, very few of them would actually say the words, "I feel like I've lost face at work." Much more likely they would say,

- I don't feel as if my boss appreciates my work.

- My colleagues don't really treat my ideas seriously.

- Some of my team members don't speak up at meetings. I don't really know what they are thinking.

- I've been passed over for promotion even though I've been recognized as one of the company's top performers.

Make no mistake—all of these comments, as well as the majority of concerns I hear, have to do with face. As an executive coach, when I hear about problems with relationships, conflicts, resistance to change, burnout, or lack of motivation, the first questions I ask often have to do with face. Interestingly enough, people's main concerns rarely have to do with not making enough money.

So let's just start right here—what is face?

Face represents one's self-esteem, self-worth, identity, reputation, status, pride, and dignity. "Face" is a universal concept that extends far beyond its origins in China. It speaks to a deeper need for dignity and acceptance, and the ways we grant dignity to one another. Understanding this universal human concept can help us make the most of our interpersonal relationships.

Think of face as a type of social currency. From that perspective, you can start to imagine how we build a supply of face with someone by continuously making deposits. You can think of it as building trust or credibility.

How do you express gratitude and appreciation to someone? How do you help them succeed? Do you compliment them and recognize them for their contributions? Do you practice empathy and put yourself in their position? Do you have their back? That is how you make a deposit.

When we need to make a withdrawal, we're careful to not "tear the face apart." We provide feedback in a way that saves face and preserves dignity. If we mistakenly cause someone to lose face, the relationship can still be saved if there are enough deposits to cover the withdrawal.

Remember three things when applying the concept of face to build deep, authentic interpersonal relationships.

1. Face is like social currency. The more you have, the easier and faster you can get things done.

2. You can build a supply of face by making deposits in the relationship, such as building trust,

keeping your promises, expressing gratitude and appreciation, and showing empathy.

3. If you accidentally cause someone to lose face, the relationship can still be saved if there are enough deposits, or trust, to cover the withdrawal.

We will be working on three aspects of face; each is a critical component to understanding how face works. The three components are: honoring face, losing face, and saving face.

Honoring face is making actual deposits of face. These are actions taken to show respect, admiration, and dignity to one or more people. Honoring face can and should be an integral part of building relationships and motivating your team or colleagues.

You can honor face for coworkers by giving their voice equal time and weight, listening to them, giving positive recognition, showing appreciation, soliciting their input, acknowledging their contributions, and showing respect for hierarchy, age, and status. The act of honoring face lifts people up, builds their confidence, and strengthens your relationships.

Losing face describes conditions where people ultimately feel devalued, humiliated, or unappreciated. Losing face occurs when something (or someone) provokes shame, fear, vulnerability, and a wide range of negative emotions in an individual or group.

Executives or managers who aren't accustomed to issues of face can inadvertently create situations where one or more parties lose face. Most of the time, the loss of face is unintentional. Here's a perfect example.

Recently I was working with a global technology company headquartered in the United States. The client asked me to speak to five engineers who were visiting from China for a week-long technical training. During the training, they sat quietly and never asked any questions. The company wanted to find out how the training was going for them.

Over lunch in the cafeteria, the engineers said little in English, but when I spoke to them in Mandarin, they immediately opened up. One complained that the American instructor had given them a 200-page technical manual as soon as they walked in the door, after a fifteen-hour flight. They had no time to review it, and it was written in English.

"How much of the training did you understand?" I asked. "About 20 percent," they replied reluctantly.

Unbeknownst to the Americans, the Chinese engineers were afraid to lose face. They needed to project an appearance of confidence and credibility. They did not want to admit that they were lost and confused. The U.S. contingent wasn't deliberately trying to cause the Chinese members to lose face, but that is exactly what happened.

Saving face is the authentic and intentional act of turning around a situation to prevent the loss of respect or dignity. To explain what it is to save face, let's go back to the meeting between the U.S. company and the Chinese engineers.

To get the U.S. and Chinese teams working more smoothly together, I recommended a few simple solutions for the American instructor: speak slowly and clearly; use diagrams and hands-on demonstrations while going over technical materials; and give the Chinese engineers time to process information and come up with questions as a group, not as individuals. In the end, the U.S. company extended the training one more week for the Chinese engineers. Both parties saved face and the training was a success.

———

I've written this book as a roadmap for executives and professionals to recognize and understand the importance of face in the workplace. We'll walk through a number of exercises on how to approach professional relationships in a way that builds up your "face savings." But on a broader level, my objective is to highlight how face is the "X factor" in all relationships, be it professional or personal.

While we all wear many hats personally and professionally, whether as a parent, friend, executive, or employee, what motivates us to move forward is usually the same set of factors: appreciation, respect, authenticity, and consideration.

And that's all about face.

CHAPTER I

Saving Face as Social Currency

W HEN YOU HEAR THE WORDS "save face," what do you think of? You might imagine someone trying to recover after saying something embarrassing. Maybe they made a misstep in the workplace and now need to repair their reputation. Egos get hurt and somehow must be mended.

The concept of "face" in many cultures extends to something far deeper. It speaks to a deeper need for dignity and acceptance, and the ways we convey that dignity to one another. The ability of people to successfully apply concepts of face as a type of social currency might be the single most integral part of establishing successful business partnerships.

Many have heard the term "face" as in "losing face." But not many understand how complex and widespread the concept is in Asia and in other cultures. Face represents a person's status and reputation in business and politics, among family and friends, in local communities—even the nation at large. The concept of face has influenced nearly every aspect of life and culture for 2,500 years.

The concept of face (*miàn zi*, in Chinese) is difficult to define because there is no English word that is a direct equivalent. "Respect" or "dignity" come close, but do not fully encapsulate all its nuance. In the historical Chinese perspective, face represents a person's reputation, credibility, and level of prestige within the family, among personal friends, and in society at large. Whatever word or phrase is used for it, in Chinese, English, or any other language, the importance of face is universal within just about every culture.

The influence of face in Asian culture typically affects three parts of society—self, community, and action.

Self relates to how an individual perceives the level of prestige they believe they've earned through their accomplishments or status within the community.

Community represents the level of respect and courtesy that should be bestowed upon someone based on their status within a business, family, or other social network.

Action corresponds to the behavior or deeds that can cause someone else to either lose or gain face.

To put it all together in terms of face, self is how you see yourself, community is how you see others, and action is what each of us does to each other that impacts face positively or negatively.

From a business perspective, the Chinese perception of face is very apparent in all levels of communications and relationships. Adherence to company hierarchy is ever present and plays a much more important role than in many Western countries. Leaders and senior managers are placed on a pedestal, and the distinction between various levels of management is clearly defined. Many leaders expect their orders to be followed without question, and when someone does not follow the intent of their leader, they are perceived as not giving the necessary prestige that the leader is owed.

While our objective here isn't to duplicate that model of business hierarchy, the concept of face is just as important in the West, and we'll be looking at how that is so throughout this book.

"THROW AWAY THE FACE"

The concept of face is so entrenched globally that common phrases about face are a normal part of everyday conversation. The Chinese phrase *diulian* translates as "throw away the face"—that is, to be so ashamed or embarrassed you feel as though you have removed your face and tossed it away. And let's not forget the Western phrase "putting your best face forward"—another way of presenting yourself with respect and honor.

The idea of saving face isn't just some theoretical concept that affects communication between groups in far-flung locations. As the following story shows, issues about face can just as easily happen in the same building.

A Picture Is Worth a Thousand Errors

My colleague Jeremy Solomons, a global leadership consultant and columnist based in Kigali, Rwanda, shared an incident involving face between the sales team and the software engineers in the same company.[1] This is Jeremy's story.

I was working with a group of software engineers in Texas and one of the engineers was working very closely with the sales manager of the company.

They met frequently and they seemed to have a good rapport. That was, until one occasion when they were doing a product review and the sales manager was in a rush to board a flight for a business meeting the next day. Much of what the two discussed in their meeting had been illustrated by the engineer on a whiteboard. Instead of taking notes, the sales manager quickly used his smartphone to take a photo of what was on the whiteboard.

During his trip, he noticed that communication with the engineering team was suddenly more formal and terse than before, and deadlines were not being met. When he brought this up with his engineering contact, the engineer initially claimed nothing was wrong. But instinct told the sales manager that something was wrong, and he found an excuse to get back and meet the engineer in person as soon as possible.

The engineering lead at first pretended nothing was wrong but, when pressed, he finally reminded the sales manager of the photograph, which contained some errors that the engineers had made and, as such, seemed like a betrayal to the team, who did not know who was going to see it.

The team felt they had lost face, and the team lead said that when the sales manager did that, "it was humiliating." The sales manager apologized sincerely and profusely, and relations between him and the engineers gradually improved again. Needless to say, he did not take any more photos!

As you go through this book, you may notice that I sprinkle a lot of anecdotes about what I've observed in my interactions with clients. It's intentional! Instead of reciting abstract theories in a vacuum, I want to show how the concept of face actually has an impact on people through real-life experiences.

Here's a terrific example of how the chief operating officer (COO) of a major corporation helped to preserve face for one of his managers when something negative happened.

Why "Saving Face" Is More Than Just a Saying

Helping someone "save face" requires empathy, kindness, and authenticity. One of my clients, Dan Nesselroth, described an experience he witnessed while working for a global company.[2]

Dan was hired by the company's finance director, who was facing a crisis. Under his watch, a frontline employee had stolen more than $100,000 in an eight-month period. Dan's manager had designed and deployed the entire cash flow process that allowed this employee to commit the fraud undetected. An optimistic and trusting person, he had included minimal anti-fraud and anti-theft controls in the design.

The case was a high-profile one; not only was it discussed in security meetings but also knowledge of it spread quickly through whispers throughout the company.

"When the theft was revealed and the scope of it ballooned with each day of the investigation, my boss felt entirely responsible and personally victimized," Dan says. "It was an example of 'losing face.'"

Soon, the company's COO planned a meeting with Dan and his manager. The stress consumed Dan's boss: He lost weight, lost sleep, and developed anxiety.

"For days he felt like a dead man walking, perhaps made even worse by the hardline reputation the COO had," Dan says.

When the day arrived, Dan and his boss waited nervously in a conference room. The COO walked in. His manager's dread and anxiety were impossible to ignore. The COO broke the tension with one sentence: "I don't care about the theft." He continued, saying that theft is unavoidable, whether one runs a hotdog stand or a multinational company. The company was insured and would be made whole. "I only want to know that you plan to review the process and fix it. And you seem well on your way, from what I can see," the COO said.

Dan reports that his manager's demeanor immediately brightened. He returned to his job with renewed energy.

The COO had saved the manager's face and did so authentically.

- He was firm but kind. Saving face requires having the
  other person's best interest in mind, understanding
  their perspective, and delivering constructive feedback.
  The COO considered the circumstances before
  making decisions. Humanity is key. Ego is the enemy.

- It's important to point out that saving face isn't the
  same as just letting someone off the hook. When a
  mistake is made, there still needs to be accountability.
  In this case, the COO communicated directly and
  clearly about his expectations and trusted that the
  financial director would see to it that the problem
  was fixed.

- He employed emotional intelligence. When he walked
  in the room, the COO was aware of the finance
  director's stress level. He "raised his antenna" and
  reacted with empathy. He was respectful, choosing
  his words carefully. He didn't make assumptions.
  He treated the finance director with decency.

- He was intentional. When having emotionally delicate
  conversations, start with the end goal in mind. Ask,
  "What is my intention? What do we want to achieve?"
  Stating your intention creates openness and breaks
  down barriers.

- He made the finance director feel worthy. The COO
  didn't demean or embarrass him. Instead, he did the
  opposite—he recognized, in front of Dan, the work the
  finance director had been doing to improve security
  measures. He acknowledged the finance director's
  self-worth and affirmed it.

- He helped the finance director overcome shame and
  embarrassment quickly and refocus his energy on

solving the problem and moving forward. He showed the finance director that he trusted him and had confidence that he would do the right thing.

Saving face is done authentically when you are intentional, respectful, and sensitive. Act with empathy and leave ego and judgment at the door. When you help someone save face in this way, you not only inspire loyalty—you also bring out the best in others, having made them feel appreciated and valued.

The act of saving face can take many forms. It may be very subtle or overt depending on the culture and environment, but it is always there.

THE BANK OF FACE

When we are attuned to face, we begin to use it as social currency. In this sense, it is possible to imagine how we build a supply of face with someone by continuously making deposits, just like a bank account. The more we deposit, the more we build trust. We express gratitude and appreciation. We compliment others and recognize them for their contributions, in public and in private. Or we empathize, putting ourselves in their place to understand their challenges. We give them and their voice equal time and weight. This is how we make a deposit.

When we need to make a withdrawal, we're careful not to "tear the face apart." We provide criticism or feedback in a way that saves face and preserves dignity. If we mistakenly cause someone to lose face, the relationship can still be saved if there are enough deposits to cover the withdrawal.

Face is also traded as currency. Global business leaders use face as a commodity, trading and borrowing face to strike mutual deals or to gain entry into one another's markets or networks. A global business leader's success depends on how he or she understands face and its crucial role in cross-cultural communication.

The more "face" you have, the easier and quicker it is to get things done.

Face as a social currency isn't solely focused on business. It matters in every interaction you have, whether it's professional or personal. Here are a couple of examples of how face works on a personal level.

You Don't Remember Me, Do You?

A good friend of mine and community influencer,
Yen Tu, shared an observation many of us can
identify with.[3] *As Yen recalls,*

When I meet someone I met a while ago, I often recognize their face but don't always recall their name. To be courteous and avoid awkwardness, I always reintroduce myself. It doesn't take anything away from me. They always seem relieved and happy that I helped them save face.

Yet on occasion, when the tables are turned, some people are not so kind or courteous. They might say, "You don't remember my name, do you?" It's a bit humiliating and, obviously, I know it doesn't have to be that way.

How a Wedding, a Truck, and a $10 Bill
Can Lead to Losing Face

Here is an example of how even the best of intentions
can lead to someone losing face on a personal level.

My husband, Wayne, and I were preparing to get married and move into a brand-new home. Wayne asked a family friend, Daniel, a friend of his father in his sixties, if he could borrow his truck to move some items from his current home to our new home.

As Wayne finished the move, he realized that he must return

the truck to Daniel quickly because he had to make it to the tailor to take measurements for his tuxedo for the wedding. When he dropped off the truck, Daniel wasn't home, so Wayne taped an envelope to the steering wheel with a thank-you note as well as $10 for the amount of gas he had used.

A few days later, he found out through his father that Daniel was very upset with him for the money left in the envelope.

Why was Daniel offended? It wasn't because he thought Wayne should have left more money. It was because Wayne left any money at all. Daniel felt he had lost face because Wayne presumed that he would want to be compensated for doing him a favor. It would have been one thing if Wayne had simply filled up the tank with $10 of gas, but leaving the money in the car was offensive and led to Daniel's loss of face.

On the level of personal relationships, whether between a parent and child, or among members of a religious congregation, the scale may be smaller but the concepts of face are equally important to how individuals relate to each other.

As an executive coach, I've worked with thousands of clients, from mid-level managers of start-ups to CEOs of Global 500 companies. Of all the challenges my clients deal with, of all the conflicts that arise in companies big and small, the most consistent characteristic missing in nearly all of these interactions is in how people deal with each other in terms of face. This book is an opportunity to share what I've learned from my experiences.

We will look at how we can *honor* face to connect with people and create positive first impressions, how we can inadvertently cause others to *lose* face in business or social situations, and, most important, how we can effectively *save* face to avoid negative consequences.

Here we go!

CHAPTER 2

How to Avoid
Losing Face

THERE'S AN OLD SAYING I remember hearing when I was growing up: Spilled water is hard to regain. When it comes to losing face, that phrase really has a lot of meaning.

Think about it—you accidentally knock a glass of water off the dining table and it spills all over the floor—if you wanted to get all that water back into the glass, how would you do it? More important, even if you managed to get all the spilled water on the ground back into the glass, at that point would you still want to drink it? Yuck. Me neither.

That "yuck" factor is the same when we're talking about face. If you do or say something that causes someone else to lose face or to feel humiliated or diminished, it's hard to completely reverse what you said or did; even if you could, the relationship has changed for the worse, at least in the short term.

Thus the best strategy is to learn how not to say or do the wrong thing, either intentionally or unintentionally. A level of empathy—putting yourself into someone else's shoes—is required to accomplish this. If you can understand how an action can impact someone else in a positive or negative way, that understanding becomes a roadmap for how you communicate to others.

Every relationship you have, and every relationship you will have, must start somewhere. The saying "You only have one chance to make a good impression" is certainly true, especially when you're dealing with face. From that perspective, understanding what can cause someone to lose face is the first thing you should consider when meeting someone for the first time, because you haven't yet developed any credibility on a personal level. You haven't deposited anything to your "face bank."

I've seen people use face for many reasons, such as elevating a business partner's status, making a positive first impression, empowering employees and building their confidence, or rewarding and recognizing team players. Yet we all face challenges in our relationships when miscommunication and misunderstanding negatively impact business deals and work relationships. The painful lesson we all must learn is that sometimes one can never regain face once it is lost. But in most cases, face can be restored through much patience, authenticity, and persistence on the part of all parties.

We'll spend time looking at strategies for avoiding behaviors that will cause someone to lose face, but let's also spend a moment to understand why it matters.

Losing face is caused when something (or someone) provokes shame, fear, vulnerability, and a wide range of negative emotions in someone else. You can cause someone to lose face by giving negative feedback in public, challenging or disagreeing with them, failing to acknowledge proper hierarchy, engaging in subtle insults, ignoring or interrupting someone, making insensitive jokes, and more.

Losing face might best be described as experiencing "undeserved shame."

In her book *The Gifts of Imperfection*, author Brené Brown writes:

> Shame is that warm feeling that washes over us, making us feel small, flawed, and never good enough. . . . Shame is the intensely painful feeling or experience of believing that we are flawed and therefore unworthy of love and belonging. . . . Shame is all about fear. We're afraid that people won't like us if they know the truth about who we are, where we come from, what we believe, how much we're struggling, or, believe it or not, how wonderful we are when soaring (sometimes it's just as hard to own our strengths as our struggles).[1]

TECHNOLOGY
AND THE LOSS OF FACE

What do these phrases with the word "face" have in common?

- Face your fear
- Face the music
- Face-to-face
- Face down

In terms of meaning, these phrases all suggest that you need to deal with the task at hand instead of avoiding the issue. How many times have you had to deal with an awkward situation and thought to yourself, "Ugh, it would just be easier to send them a text or email instead of dealing with this in person." I know I have.

Now apply that same awkward feeling about dealing with something and toss in the immediacy of technology in all its forms—emails, texts, social media, and direct messages. You can see how the potential for losing face multiplies dramatically with the indirectness and casual nature of technology. Technology makes it easy to avoid uncomfortable situations, and, beyond that, without the subtleties of body language and tone of voice, meaning and nuance can easily become misconstrued or seemingly offensive.

FACE-TO-FACE
(TO SAVE FACE)

Technology has revolutionized the way we consume and distribute information. There's an immediacy that comes from being able to get whatever information you need, whether it's a text message from a friend saying they'll be late to a party, invites that just show up on your online calendar, or even a reminder on your digital sprinkler telling you there's a leak somewhere in your yard.

While having all that information literally at our fingertips has certainly given us more control, there's also a real downside to having a digital wall between us and the people we communicate with, especially in terms of face: a loss in civility.

There's a certain loss of graciousness in our digital communication, whether we're talking about email or texts. There is no body language authentically expressed in texts, and don't even get me started on the war zone of social media.

A recent article published by NPR discussed at length how perfect strangers or even family members can come into conflict with the feeling of entitlement that people have about chiming in on any given topic without considering the impact of their words. When two family members started a discussion about gun control, the discussion got so heated and distraught that the members ended up "unfriending" each other. One of them later said, "If this whole topic would have happened in person, nobody would have walked away."[2]

One of my clients shared her experience with cyber bullying coming from her own friends and family.

CYBER BULLYING

My client Melissa, a twenty-five-year-old Harvard graduate working at a small nonprofit, was raised in Lebanon. She lives in a close-knit community where 90 percent of her community are also from Lebanon. In her high school class, she was the only student to be accepted into Harvard. You'd think that accomplishment would be a point of pride!

Instead, her schoolmates and their parents shamed and bullied her for "showing off" when she posted some pictures of herself on Harvard's campus on her Facebook page. Instead of being able to celebrate her success, she completely stopped posting anything on social media. She had lost face and actually felt ashamed for her success. After graduating from Harvard, she wanted to give back to the community and started working for a local nonprofit. The same "friends" on Facebook continued to shame her on social media by belittling her career, with one person commenting, "Was that all you could do?"

Hanna Rosin, in her article "The End of Empathy," describes, through various studies, how our current generation has lost the ability to feel empathy for others. People no longer feel it is necessary to feel what it's like to be in someone else's shoes, and are much more inclined to feel empathy with those they already support or have an affinity with. She writes about a study done by Sara Konrath, an associate professor at Indiana University:

> More students say it's not their problem to help people in trouble, not their job to see the world from someone else's perspective. By 2009, on all the standard measures, Konrath found, young people on average measure 40 percent less empathetic than my own generation—40 percent![3]

Combine that with the effects of technology on our current communications, and you quickly see how an "every man for himself" sensibility can create issues. Yet that is exactly the wrong direction for us to be going if we are going to develop strong relationships with our peers and business associates by saving or preserving face.

Empathy and face are intertwined. You can't really have one without the other. Let's think for a moment about what the word "empathy" really means.

A quick Google search of the word comes up with *The ability to understand and share the feelings of another.*

Now, think about that in the context of saving face. The goal when relating to others is to avoid conveying undeserved shame to them so that they don't lose face. Particularly when dealing with someone whose background is unlike yours, the challenge is, how can you avoid doing or saying something that might cause them to lose face when you don't know what it's like to walk in their shoes?

Let's take perhaps the clearest example of this type of challenge—working with others from a cross-cultural perspective. While the following example is about working with groups who are likely from another country and speaking another language, the concepts here are relevant when you are working with anyone or any group that you aren't familiar with.

FOUR WAYS TO SHED THE "UGLY AMERICAN" IMAGE AND SUCCEED IN GLOBAL BUSINESS

These techniques will help you build trust with your international colleagues.

We all have a mental picture of the so-called "ugly American"—brash and arrogant, with an ethnocentric belief in America's singular greatness. When ugly Americans travel, they tout Big Macs over local cuisine and offer firm hand-shakes no matter what the local greeting customs are.

The phrase emerged around the middle of the last century, made popular by a 1958 novel and a 1963 film starring Marlon Brando.[4] In my travels around the world as an executive coach, I have observed that this cultural stereotype persists in the minds of many of my international clients.

For example, a Chinese executive I know remarked that Americans tend to start sentences with "I," as in, "I had excellent results last quarter," or "I found a great place for us all to have dinner." The executive doubted these American colleagues really deserved sole credit. In China, the collective is generally considered more important than the individual.

When working across cultures, sometimes it's less important to be "right" and more important to be aware of the impression you create. You may be exhibiting "ugly American" traits without realizing it. Even I have done it—and I was born and raised in Taiwan! Living in the United States since 1985, I've naturally taken on American behaviors and attitudes—like thinking and talking fast. That's good, right? Well, not always.

I once led a leadership seminar for a multinational company. A Korean manager raised his hand to speak, and I gave him the floor. His English was good, but not quite native. When he paused for a few seconds, I assumed that he had finished, and I moved on to the next person.

My assumption was wrong. It turned out that he was not done at all, and he was furious that I had cut him off mid-thought. He was actually about to leave the conference, but just before he could slip away, one of his coworkers pulled me aside to tell me what was going on.

Immediately, I asked to speak with the manager privately. His face reddening, he told me that my insensitive interruption was a gesture of disrespect that caused him to lose face. I told him that I understood why he felt that way, and I deeply regretted offending him. He agreed to stay, and he turned out to be an enthusiastic contributor for the rest of the conference. In the end, he gave the event an excellent evaluation.

The following four tips will help you avoid (or recover gracefully from) communication pitfalls like these when working across cultures.

1. **Respect the hierarchy.** Americans tend to be informal and egalitarian. It's a badge of honor for a CEO or a politician to seem like a "regular guy." In many countries, business is much more hierarchical—aimed at creating a culture of respect and stability. In Japan, for example, disagreeing with a superior is off limits. On the other hand, in countries like Australia and Canada, people tend to be suspicious of formality. Know the expectations of your international counterparts and be prepared to adjust.

2. **Raise your cultural antenna.** Interacting with another culture requires preparation. Read as much as you can about that environment and learn about the people you'll be working with. I recommend finding a cultural informant who can tell you what gifts are suitable, what traditions to observe, and so on. A simple commitment to stay alert is important, too. When I fly to another country, at some point during the flight I imagine a switch in my mind. When I flip it on, I have a heightened awareness of the different world I'm entering.

3. **Avoid irritating phrases.** My international clients complain about the tendency of Americans to interrupt, their

arrogant assumption that they already know the answers, their heavy use of acronyms and jargon, and the way they sometimes fail to say exactly what they mean. Sarcastic comments such as "That's just great!" might come off as sincere to someone unfamiliar with American culture and idioms. Non-native English speakers can also struggle with interpreting vague answers like "I can't say," or "I'm not sure." And they don't particularly like being asked, "Do you understand?," because it feels condescending.

4. **Use the Platinum Rule.** The Golden Rule states, "Treat others as you would like to be treated." But that can backfire if other people don't want the same things you do (which is entirely possible when the person comes from a very different place). Dr. Tony Alessandra has come up with what he calls the Platinum Rule: "Treat others the way they want to be treated."[5] For that to work, you have to find out what others want and value. To that end, I find it helps to inquire with an open mind—and leave all your assumptions behind. I was recently hired by a large private equity firm in Asia to coach a promising executive. He seemed to fit all the Asian stereotypes: quiet, reserved, and hierarchical. And yet he actually grew up in New York City and feels a great affinity for American culture.

Don't let any of your business ventures fall apart due to miscommunication and damaged trust. Wherever in the world you happen to travel and whatever foreign cultures you encounter, be sincere, curious, and willing to listen—really listen—to someone whose background is nothing like yours. Your next deal may depend on it.

Cross-cultural specialist Kiyoshi Matsumoto writes on the differences of face between the West and Asia, specifically Japan.

"Western face" is a more self-oriented and individualistic pride or ego, and is more about how one is viewed by others. "Japanese face" is about how one treats others, not about the self, and can be given or earned. It can be also taken away or lost.

His advice on how to engage with the Japanese?

It is recommended to take John Wayne's acting advice: "*Talk low, talk slow, and don't talk too much.*" In other words one should act like one is trying to feed a nut to a nervous squirrel—approach at an angle, do not attract too much attention and make no sudden moves!"[6]

Even as an executive coach, it's my job to practice what I preach. Actually, I couldn't be effective at what I do without doing just that. Here's how I applied these ideas with one of my clients.

Bruce Lee to the rescue

I once had to coach a high-level personal computer company executive, whom we'll call John, who was having some difficulties with his colleagues. I was charged with doing a 360-degree feedback on John to help him improve the way he communicated with his peers. A 360-degree feedback is when we interview peers, superiors, and staff on the person being coached to better understand how the person is being perceived by those they are working with every day. It's a confidential process to encourage everyone to speak freely.

While John's feedback showed that as the company's chief procurement officer he was skillful with his negotiations with vendors and able to save the company millions of dollars, his colleagues found him to be difficult.

When we discussed the survey results, John became quiet as he heard more and more about what his peers and colleagues thought of him. Many of them said that John would dismiss their ideas or answer their questions with a simple "no," without providing any other thoughts or concerns, which made them feel inadequate. To them, he came off as negative and arrogant.

I asked him some questions about his approach to his work, and John shared that he was a fan of kung fu novels and saw a correlation between his work and how ancient warriors dealt with their own challenges. Perhaps subconsciously, he was treating his colleagues as though they were enemies, instead of being part of a team, which is what they were. Once I understood John's outlook on his work, I incorporated his interests in a way he might better accept them. I presented the following suggestions to him.

Face your feedback. John resisted much of the feedback at first, arguing that he knew the job so well it was a waste of time to explain himself to his colleagues. In his mind, it was his job to cut off bad ideas quickly, no explanation needed. "Wait a minute," I said. "Are your coworkers your enemies?" "Well, they're annoying," was his answer.

Over the next few coaching sessions, I worked hard to convince John that his colleagues were allies, not enemies, and that he should accept their feedback. It would take courage to face his failures, but he would be better for it in the end, I told him.

He eventually began to see the damage he'd done by treating the people around him as opponents. Extending the kung fu analogy, he realized that his ruthless efficiency was actually creating more enemies—a strategic error. He didn't need to change his inner beliefs about the value of hard work and loyalty to the company. He did need to change his communication style.

As Bruce Lee has said, *"To know oneself is to study oneself in action with another person."*[7]

Admit your mistakes. The next step in the coaching process was for John to meet with the people who gave him feedback. He was reluctant to admit his shortcomings in front of his peers, but he did. He thanked his critics for their honesty and told them he had a plan to improve.

"I'm not going to say *no* immediately from now on," he promised. "We are partners on the same team. I'm going to ask questions, listen, and come up with win-win solutions with you."

Bruce Lee has observed, "*Mistakes are always forgivable, if one has the courage to admit them.*"[8]

Pick a new habit and practice it constantly. Changing behavior is a hard, daily practice. You have to keep your goal in mind all the time, through every interaction, so that your new habit will take root.

Despite his initial reluctance, John proved to be a good coachee. The people around him began to notice him becoming kinder and gentler. His new attitude spread to his team, too. He faced a big test in a high-level meeting, when a manager asked him to do something he felt was unreasonable and nearly impossible. Instead of immediately saying no, he took a breath.

"Let me explain why it can't be done," he said, and then offered an alternative solution. He made a point to smile and even cracked a joke. His coworkers were surprised and pleased—and happy to accept his alternative plan.

Bruce Lee again: "*To hell with circumstances; I create opportunities.*"[9]

I have seen many clients use these principles with great success. Having the courage to know yourself, the humility to accept your shortcomings, and the discipline to work toward positive change can help you, too, wherever in the world you happen to live.

I was using empathy when I tried to put myself in John's shoes. Once I did that, I could share information that would help him put himself in someone else's shoes. That helped John understand where his colleagues were coming from, which ultimately helped his colleagues save face.

No one wants to spill milk. Now that we know what losing face is all about, we can use the tools of putting ourselves into someone else's shoes, having empathy, and not letting technology warp our communication—these are all ways to avoid spilling milk.

Oh, and by the way, thanks, Bruce! I owe you one.

CHAPTER 3

Authentic Acts
of Saving and
Honoring Face

OW DO YOU FEEL when you're checking out of a store
and someone behind the counter says, "Have a nice
day"? Do you get a little shimmy in your step? Does
your day get a little brighter? After all, someone you
likely never met and may never meet again made the effort to
wish you a nice day! No? Ever wonder why that is?

A quick look at the term "Have a nice day" on Wikipedia
finds:

> Since it is often uttered by service employees to customers
> at the end of a transaction, its repetitious and dutiful usage
> has resulted in the phrase developing, according to some jour-
> nalists and scholars, a cultural connotation of impersonality,
> lack of interest, passive-aggressive behavior, or sarcasm. Other
> critics argue that it is a parting platitude that comes across as
> pretended.[1]

It "comes across as pretended." It's an emotionless comment to fill up the silence. It doesn't mean anything because
they didn't really mean it. It's inauthentic.

Now think of how this lack of authenticity factors into

saving face. How can you ever convey to someone that their work is of value, that they should be proud of their accomplishments, and that they are to be trusted if you don't really mean it? The *authentic* act of "saving face" requires a positive intention and understanding the other person's frame of reference without judgment. Without positive intention and acceptance, the act of "saving face" can be perceived as manipulative, superficial, or phony. As author Brené Brown says, "Authenticity is not something we have or don't have. It's a practice—a conscious choice of how we want to live. . . . It's about the choice to show up and be real. The choice to be honest. The choice to let our true selves be seen."[2]

Here are some ways to put "saving face" into action in an authentic way.

- **Preserving dignity for others.** Dignity is the state or quality of being worthy of honor or respect.

- **Showing compassion.** Pema Chödrön observes, "Compassion is not a relationship between the healer and the wounded. It's a relationship between equals. Only when we know our own darkness well can we be present with the darkness of others. Compassion becomes real when we recognize our shared humanity."[3] And Brené Brown notes that "the heart of compassion is really acceptance. The better we are at accepting ourselves and others, the more compassionate we become. . . . We can be compassionate and accepting while we hold people accountable for their behaviors. We can, and, in fact, it's the best way to do it."[4]

- **Caring.** Good intentions are not enough. You need to care about how your actions *impact* others. You need to care about how people are treated, and how they feel. You need to care about building positive relationships

that lift people up instead of putting them down. You
don't manage by fear. You aim to preserve the dignity
of others and enable them to do their best work.

- **Winning.** You strive to achieve the best outcomes for
  all parties involved. It is not win/lose, not win/win,
  but winning all around. Achieving this may require
  compromise, negotiation, powerful questions, authentic
  conversations, and creative solutions.

- **Being firm but kind (benevolent).** Have the other person's
  best interest in mind, listen and understand their
  perspective, hold people accountable, give constructive
  feedback. Consider their circumstance before making
  decisions. Humanity is key. Ego is the enemy.

- **Using emotional intelligence.** Raise your antenna.
  Be self-aware, and be able to accept and adapt to
  another's frame of reference.

- **Creating psychological safety.** Make others feel heard,
  understood, and valued. Create a safe space for people
  to speak, contribute, share, disagree, and challenge.
  In a safe space, people can show compassion, empathy,
  and sensitivity.

- **Being civil.** Be respectful. Be impeccable with your words.
  Think before you speak. Avoid making assumptions or
  taking anything personally. Treat others with decency
  and civility, without judgment.

- **Being intentional.** Start with the end goal in mind.
  Ask, "What is my intention? What do we want to
  achieve?" State your intention repeatedly to create
  openness and break down barriers.

- **Following the Platinum Rule.** Treat others as *they* would
  like to be treated, not how *you* would like to be treated.

- **Practicing "straight talk."** Say what needs to be said to the right person at the appropriate time and place—respectfully, clearly, and accurately. The opposite of straight talk is either "blunt talk" or "safe talk," which cause others to lose face (see chapter 10).

- **Being inclusive.** Saving face promotes a sense of belonging, not just fitting-in. When people feel they belong, they are more open, more relaxed, more productive, and happier.

- **Promoting worthiness.** Saving face is about self-worth and making others feel worthy. You extend your self-worth by connecting with others and making them feel appreciated, valued, and loved.

Being authentic isn't just a means to an end. In terms of saving face, it is the main factor for maintaining dignity.

Carnegie Deli and That Pastrami Sandwich

About twenty years ago, I visited New York City and went to the famous Carnegie Deli for lunch. I couldn't finish their giant deli sandwich, so I took half of it to go in a brown bag. As I stepped out of the restaurant, I saw a homeless man sitting on the sidewalk near the restaurant. I approached him and offered, "Would you like to have half of this deli sandwich? I haven't touched it." He looked at me for a few seconds and said, "What kind is it?" I was surprised by that reaction and said politely, "It's pastrami." He nodded and took it. I turned around and kept walking. A few seconds later, the man ran after me and tapped my shoulder, saying, "Hey, lady, this is for you. It is a trade." He handed me a coupon for a show in the city and walked away.

He didn't want to receive a favor and not give something in return. He preserved his own dignity and saved face. I respect that.

Authenticity is just part of the equation. In the list above, let's look at the idea of emotional intelligence and how it affects face and dignity. Let's look at the following example.

HOW DOES IT FEEL
TO LOSE FACE?

Let me try explaining a concept to you: Sir Isaac Newton theorized that in order for an object to move forward or accelerate, some force must be applied to it. Of course, friction and gravity play significant roles in determining the amount of force needed to move an object. Newton's basic formula for this effect is

$$force = mass \times acceleration$$

Robert Goddard, a pioneer in rocket propulsion, is credited with developing the first liquid fuel rocket; he also theorized that in order to more easily break through Earth's gravity, multistage rockets could be used to reduce the weight and send payloads into orbit more efficiently. In addition, he was one of the first to successfully implement three-axis controls on his flights.

Got it? I can imagine that at this moment, you're thinking, What the heck are you talking about, and what does this have to do with face? Just go with me for a minute.

I'm no rocket scientist (I was waiting to use that line) and I assume you aren't either. But you can see that I didn't give you any context before I "launched" into my little description on the origins of rocket propulsion, and I included phrases like "three-axis controls" with the assumption that you already knew what I was talking about.

Now, let's assume that I've presented you with a 200-page report on rocket propulsion concepts, filled with highly technical terms, acronyms you'd never heard of, and I've begun providing a highly technical overview of the report using very few illustrations or hands-on examples, and I'm assuming that you are completely up to speed on the basic concepts of rocket propulsion. One last thing—both the report and my entire presentation are done in Swahili.

After a day of this, how would you feel? If I asked everyone in the room if they had any questions, what kind of question would you ask, with everyone else in the room watching? Based on this extreme example, it's very possible that you wouldn't know enough to even ask a relevant question. You can see that people put into such a situation—particularly if they are from cultures in Asia that place a heavy emphasis on respect, honor, and a need to project competency—might easily feel flummoxed, overwhelmed, and even undeservedly shamed that they aren't immediately able to keep up. Understanding the problems inherent in a situation like this is a part of emotional intelligence.

This example actually isn't as far-fetched or extreme as it sounds. Scenes like this happen every day in international business. In fact, I witnessed a nearly identical situation just a while ago. I brought up this story briefly in the Introduction, but I want to expand on it here because it really does show how—as any stand-up comedian will tell you—you need to read your room.

A couple of years ago, I traveled to a company in Arizona, arriving on a Wednesday to deliver a two-day global leadership training.

At the end of the first day, an executive of the company mentioned that a group of engineers from China was visiting for a week of training. Their technical training was scheduled for five days, Monday to Friday. The executive noted that the Chinese engineers were very quiet during the training and, when given the opportunity, asked very few questions. He asked if I could meet with the group for lunch on Thursday to get a sense of how things were going. I told him I'd be happy to do it.

As I walked into the cafeteria the next day, I greeted the group and we exchanged pleasantries. After a few minutes, I asked them how the training was going. A number of them pensively looked at each other before softly replying, "It's okay."

Sensing that something deeper was going on, I spoke to them in their native Chinese and probed a bit more. After a few more minutes, they opened up to me.

One engineer said, "It's been difficult to follow, because the company handed us a 200-page manual right when we walked in, and didn't give us any time to review it before the instructor started his presentation. The manual is very technical and it's all in English." I asked them how much of the training they understood, and they replied reluctantly, "About 20 percent."

The engineer went on to say, "Occasionally, when the instructor asks if we have any questions, we just don't know enough to ask a question that could help us."

This is a perfect example of how the concept of face applies when two groups are working on different wavelengths, which can cause confusion and put up obstacles to working efficiently.

The company that set up the training didn't fully consider how to adapt their training methods to a group that was unlike those they normally work with. As a result, the training created an atmosphere for the visiting Chinese engineers in which they were hesitant to admit that they were completely lost and were unsure about how to get back up to speed. The company didn't consider the needs of this particular team.

I asked the Chinese engineers for their permission to

share the feedback with the instructor and the sponsoring executive. They asked me not to link the feedback with any specific names so that no one would "lose face." I agreed.

I spent some time with the group to see how we could salvage the training session. Here's what we came up with.

- Ask the instructor to speak more slowly and take additional time on complex technical concepts.

- As before, ask the group if they have questions, but also give the group time to talk among themselves, make sure they are all on the same page, and come up with questions as a group so that no one is singled out.

- Provide all documentation well in advance so the group has time to study and prepare ahead of time. It is important to provide graphic illustrations whenever possible as part of the documentation.

- Whenever possible, have the instructor provide a hands-on experience so the ideas being taught are more realistic and less conceptual.

After I shared these suggestions with the company, the training session was extended a week and it became far more productive for both the company and the Chinese team members.

You might ask, "If the Chinese group was having such a tough time, why didn't they just bring up these issues right in the beginning so they could work things out sooner?"

It all has to do with saving face. While the inability of the Chinese group to fully understand the instruction was completely due to the ineffectiveness of the training methods, the group was hesitant to admit that they were completely lost, because such an admission, while certainly understandable in this situation, was still a point of embarrassment for them.

This example involves a group of Chinese engineers, but saving face really extends to all cultures. In my initial example, even if the entire presentation on rocket propulsion were done in English, the important distinction is that you were suddenly thrust into a situation where you had no context or experience that you could apply toward your understanding. If you were watching the presentation as part of a large group, you'd be put into a position where, if you really wanted to get a better understanding of the topic, you would have to admit to everyone that you were clueless, and that's never a place anyone wants to be in. Being emotionally intelligent helps avoid these kinds of situations.

Saving face is not just a method to use when problems arise. It can and should be an integral part of motivating your team and showing that you value them. It pays dividends right from the start.

When you think of the term "face-saving," as in "It was a face-saving gesture," it usually relates to someone taking action to keep someone else from feeling humiliated or devalued. While that's certainly one aspect of saving face, a very proactive, positive aspect of it can also serve a constructive purpose. Take a look at these motivational strategies that are ways of "honoring" face.

FACE-FRIENDLY MOTIVATIONAL STRATEGIES—HONORING FACE

Creativity and genuine appreciation go a long way when it comes to motivating workers whose main capital is knowledge.

As an executive coach, I have a unique vantage point on what goes on inside companies—and the brains of the people leading them. Working with clients one-on-one as they navigate major conflicts gives me a deep understanding of their motivations.

Whether they're in Singapore or Kansas, I've found that knowledge workers share certain characteristics. As Daniel Pink pointed out in his brilliant 2009 book, *Drive: The Surprising Truth about What Motivates Us*, the traditional workplace carrots of pay and promotion go only so far. Knowledge workers, whose jobs require independent thinking and critical analysis, need to flex their intellectual muscles and get recognition for doing so (as Pink argues, it comes down to autonomy, mastery, and purpose). Studies have shown that the main reasons knowledge workers leave jobs are lack of recognition, lack of involvement, and poor management. Money is rarely the issue.

Much as authenticity is the key to saving face, it's just as important when honoring face. Here are some strategies for honoring face that have worked wonders for my clients.

Get creative about public recognition. Years ago, I worked with a senior leader at a California company who wanted to motivate his management team but didn't have the budget to hand out raises. He noticed that people who came into his office always commented on a jar of rocks on his desk, which he'd picked up running on a nearby beach. One day he had the brainstorm of giving them as gifts. When a member of his team did a great job on something, he'd write a thank-you note and include one of the beach rocks from his collection. These unique and highly personal tokens began to take on an almost mythic status among his employees. If you got one of his rocks, you'd really done something special.

Allow flexible working hours. When I walked into the office of Alibaba Group, the Chinese online retailer, I was struck by the colorful tents set up between desks. I learned that during busy periods workers sleep in them. At many American technology companies, it's not uncommon to hear of employees leaving the office at eight in the morning after working all night. Given the demands of corporate life in a competitive environment, give employees the opportunity to choose their hours—as long as they get their work done, of course.

Ask them to mentor, coach, or teach. Asking someone to mentor a new hire is a signal that he or she is a valued company ambassador capable of conveying the company's core culture and values. Asking one employee to coach another has to be done sensitively (it won't work so well if the two workers are competitors, for example). But done right, it can prove as inspiring to the coach as the person getting coached. At one company I worked with, a manager created lunchtime learning sessions, in which an employee with a particular expertise taught a workshop to his or her peers. These votes of confidence go a long way toward retaining smart, dedicated employees.

Add challenge and visibility. For trained and highly skilled workers, being asked to do something more challenging is a special distinction. If you see an employee lagging, try upping the game with a harder task or a presentation in front of more influential people.

Offer face time with a key player. Many workers wonder if the senior leadership notices their efforts, or whether they're simply cogs in the corporate machine. A breakfast or coffee with a CEO or some other key company player can reassure workers that their contributions are valued and recognized at the highest level.

Many of the examples we offer show how saving face can overcome a challenge, but that isn't the only benefit of saving or honoring face. It can be used preemptively, to engage a team, to motivate them, and to encourage them.

CHAPTER 4

Saving Face
for the Wrong Reason

W E'VE NOW DEFINED what saving face is about and noted that it has to be done authentically. But that's not the end of the story. Let's take a look at a hypothetical.

John is in charge of the marketing division of a large multinational firm. One of John's team members, Cory, has been with the company for only a few months, but in that time he's impressed John with his positive attitude and his work ethic. The only problem—Cory's last two sales forecasts have been wildly off, and they seem to be based on information that either has been compiled incorrectly or is from another sales region altogether.

Before the next sales forecast is due, John decides to sit down with Cory to go through his preliminary figures. Before he does so, John goes through the numbers and corrects some obvious mistakes in the report. He brings the updated report to the meeting with Cory and then:

1. Tells Cory how much he appreciates his effort.

2. Tells him that if he needs any help in the future, his door is always open.

3. Talks to Cory about some other projects he thinks
   Cory could really help with.

Cory feels good. John feels good. No one lost face. Mission
accomplished, right? Not exactly. As I'm sure many of you
spotted, John never brought up the issue of the sales forecast
figures and never worked with Cory to help him figure out
how to do them properly in the future.

My point is, one of the objectives of saving face is to preserve dignity, but preserving dignity without dealing with a
real problem serves no purpose at all. Along with knowing
what saving face is, we also need to know what it is not. Saving face is *not*:

- **Being soft.** It is a soft skill that is *hard* to do.

- **Avoiding conflict.** Conflict avoidance is bad for business.
  One clue that a meeting is avoiding conflict is if the least
  bit of discomfort causes someone to suggest that you
  "take it offline." This, of course, triggers the meeting-
  after-the-meeting phenomenon—another hallmark of a
  conflict-avoidant culture. Avoiding conflict means that an
  organization fails to make the difficult trade-offs required
  to prioritize, which leads to overwhelming workloads.
  Avoiding conflict means tolerating someone's poor
  performance, which means other employees have to pick
  up the slack. Avoiding conflict means that it's not safe to
  express dissent or frustration, which means that stress
  and resentment build. The end result is that issues start
  piling up when they aren't dealt with in a timely manner.
  Banking conflict only ends up building a wall that no
  one wants to climb over. The ability to get issues on the
  table and work through them constructively is critical to
  having a healthy culture.

- **Using safe talk or lip service.** Saving face doesn't mean that you dance around the issue, drop hints to avoid confrontation, or minimize discomfort.

- **Tolerating bad behavior or poor performance.**

- **Being afraid to say no.** Saving face is pointless if you end up saying "yes" to everything just to avoid confrontation. Inefficiencies pop up because employees come up with unproductive work-arounds rather than dealing with an unproductive system or team member. Instead of working through a problem, frustrations and resentment bubble up. In today's work environment, where we aspire to the happiness of our employees and avoid conflict, working through an issue sometimes seems to have no place in our engagement with others. It's not about not saying "no"—it's about *how* you say it.

- **Covering up your own mistakes and avoiding accountability.** When mistakes happen, take ownership of your actions. Do not point fingers at others. It takes integrity and courage to own up to your own mistakes and take actions to correct them. That's leadership.

There is a broad spectrum in how people address conflict. On one end is not addressing conflict at all, and on the other end is being brutally honest about it, as if that were a virtue. Unless someone is guilty of intentionally doing something shameful, confronting someone in a way that demeans their sense of self-worth accomplishes nothing other than hurt feelings. Saving face effectively means navigating the middle of the spectrum—addressing an issue honestly in a way that preserves dignity. It's the hardest way to go, but also the one that leads to the best outcome.

Confronting someone who either needs feedback or addressing an ongoing issue—that's really the most obvious situation where saving face needs to be applied effectively. But Saving Face, or just the need to save face, has many applications other than just dealing with an immediate issue.

Kim Scott wrote about her experience of working at Apple along with Steve Jobs, and how the debate that leads to constructive ideas can often be stifled when face is not maintained in a group dynamic.

> Steve Jobs once told the story of going over to a neighbor's house as a kid. The neighbor asked him to collect rocks in the yard. Steve collected a few and handed them over to the neighbor, who threw them into a tin can with some liquid and sandy grit, shut the lid, and turned on a motor which rotated the can. Over a terrible racket, the neighbor asked Steve to come back the next day. When he returned, the neighbor turned off the rock tumbler and pulled out the stones. Steve was astounded to see how beautiful they had become, polished and shiny.
>
> Years later, he likened debate on a team to that rock tumbler. There's a lot of noise, a lot of friction, but out of that process, sometimes painful, come these beautiful polished stones. Both the work and the people who do the work get polished.[1]

How do you create a culture of debate without creating a "mean" culture or destroying team relationships? After all, you don't want to leave the rock tumbler on so long that there is nothing left but dust.

It's all too tempting as the boss to just make a decision to spare your team the pain of debate. Often, your team will beg you to "just decide." But if you do, you'll make worse decisions and get worse results. Your team's ability to resolve conflict and make decisions will atrophy. Despite the noise and friction, open debate creates a healthier atmosphere on a team than does repressed disagreement or backstabbing.

The one point in Scott's article that most stood out was Jobs's ability to set aside who was right or wrong. She writes that in an interview,

> Steve Jobs said, "I don't mind being wrong. And I'll admit that I'm wrong a lot. It doesn't really matter to me too much. What matters to me is that we do the right thing." Again, this willingness to be proven wrong points to the importance of pulling ego out of a debate. Rather than proving he was right, Steve Jobs used debate to collaborate to get to the right answer. Even though he was at first vehemently opposed to launching iTunes on the Windows platform, he allowed himself to be overruled. If he hadn't, the iPod would not have seen the success it did; it's likely there'd be no iPhone, no iPad. If you win every debate, your team will stop debating you. You've got to be willing to be wrong.[2]

Anyone who has followed Steve Jobs's career and history knows that he wasn't afraid of conflict. Those closest to him, like Tim Cook and Jony Ive, have recounted how Jobs had a reverence for getting the best ideas out of a group, regardless of who got credit.

Jobs's analogy of the rock tumbler and the care necessary to have the rocks come out shiny and smooth applies to a debate in which the best ideas come from a team where each team member is valued for their input and has the freedom and confidence to contribute.

It doesn't matter if the process of developing a solution to a problem is at times rough, cacophonous, and challenging, as long as everyone involved knows that their contribution is valued and they are all working toward a common goal. If it were easy, it really wouldn't be much of a challenge.

Using the rock tumbler analogy, it can feel like you're being "put through the grinder" while working to save and protect the face of others.

CHAPTER 5

Psychological Safety, Innovation, . . . and Face

OW THAT WE'VE ESTABLISHED what face is and is not, let's look at the kind of work environment you can create when face is preserved as a part of the overall culture, and how that culture can lead to positive results.

Our environment, whether we're talking about work or our personal lives, is filled with contrasts. There are differences in ethnicity, culture, generations, languages, gender, and time (if you work with teams outside your area). Without the right atmosphere, where diverse ideas and attitudes are accepted, conflicts can easily arise, either intentionally or unintentionally.

Don't worry—I'm not asking anyone to create a perfect, peaceful, mountaintop retreat environment for people to do their best work. Utopia isn't the goal. After all, if an environment free of distractions and noise were the key to success, I doubt that so many people would be meeting up at their nearest Starbucks. It's not about the place. It's about whether people feel welcomed *in* that place.

Research has shown that when an environment of psychological safety is created—a culture where people feel respected and supported—they feel safe enough to step out of their comfort zones.[1] At the very heart of creating psychological safety in an organization is the ability to honor face, save face, and avoid situations where someone loses face. Psychological safety is the end result of successfully implementing face strategies.

In order to get a team to start thinking that "there might be another way," they have to feel secure enough that, if they step out on a limb, their ideas won't be rejected or, even worse, ridiculed. If you can create that type of atmosphere, then you will be leading a team that embraces innovation.

Creating an environment of psychological safety is just another way of preserving face. When we are careful to preserve the dignity and face of others, we create psychological safety in an environment that also reduces the fear and negativity that lead to lost face.

WHAT IS THE SECRET OF GOOGLE'S BEST TEAMS?

When Google studied its most successful teams, the company discovered the secret isn't in the "who"—it's in the "how."[2]

When Google's People Operations department (their version of human resources) set out to study what made their most high-performing teams tick, they were surprised by the results. It turns out that it isn't a magic combination of skill sets, individual traits, educational backgrounds, or even cultural backgrounds that makes a team successful. It is something more.

Over the span of two years, Google studied the attributes of more than 180 of the company's teams. They interviewed more than 200 workers around the globe. They found that a team's success didn't depend on who was on it—it depended on how the workers felt as members of the team.

How the team members interacted, structured their work, and viewed their contributions had the greatest impact on a team's success.

Many dynamics contributed to employees feeling this way on their high-performing teams. But Google discovered one to be the most crucial: the dynamic of "psychological safety."

What is psychological safety?

Harvard professor Amy Edmondson and coauthor Kathryn S. Roloff define psychological safety as follows:

> Psychological safety, or the belief that one will not be rejected or humiliated in a particular setting or role, describes a climate in which people feel free to express work-relevant thoughts and feelings. In psychologically-safe environments, people believe that if they make a well-intentioned mistake, others will not think less of them for it, nor will they resent or penalize them for asking for help, information or feedback. Psychological safety thus fosters the confidence to take interpersonal risks, allowing oneself and one's colleagues to learn and focus on collective goals and problem prevention rather than on self-protection.[3]

Psychological safety is a state of being. It's the feeling team members have when they believe they can take risks without feeling insecure or embarrassed. They feel safe enough to be vulnerable in front of one another.

When workers feel it is safe for them to take risks, they are not afraid to fail. They are open to trying something new and to challenging the status quo. The result is that they become more creative and innovative. They perform at a higher level because they strive for the best as a team—instead of striving to protect themselves as individuals.

How do you create psychological safety?
Psychological safety isn't the responsibility of leaders alone—
it takes an entire team to co-create this environment. Here
are three steps to start the shift.

1. **Establish taking turns in conversations.** When a team
functions in harmony, each member speaks an equal amount
of time. One or two people do not dominate the discussion.
Each person feels they get the opportunity to contribute, and
no one holds back. This balance doesn't happen automati-
cally—it takes intention and practice. Often, it's as simple as
being aware of who isn't speaking and welcoming them into
the conversation. But there are other approaches, too. I work
with a leader who has discovered an ingenious way to achieve
this balance. If he, or anyone else on the team, notices someone hasn't contributed, they hand that person a small rock.
If someone has the rock, it's their turn to speak. The rock is
passed quietly, discreetly, and is a way of saying, "I'd love to
hear what you think."

2. **Self-check negative behavior.** If a team has a history of
destructive behaviors—such as sarcastic comments, demean-
ing remarks, or other micro-inequities—it's a leader's job to
call out those behaviors and discourage them. Then it's up
to the entire team to constantly monitor one another—and
themselves—to make sure these behaviors don't pop up. If
they do, they can erode relationships and impede progress
toward psychological safety. A team functions best when individual ego is out of the room and there's mutual respect
among all the members.

3. **Maintain high social sensitivity.** Much of what we communicate is nonverbal. We convey as much information in

our tone of voice, facial expressions, and body language as we do in our words. When a team has a culture of mutual respect, the people on it have a heightened awareness of what their colleagues are communicating. They are sensitive to how other team members feel and react. This is a key component of psychological safety.

Google's research turned up an additional fascinating fact: According to Julia Rozovsky from Google's People Operations, the workers on teams with psychological safety also perform more strongly as individuals.[4] They are less likely to leave the company and more likely to embrace diverse ideas, bring in more revenue, and be rated as effective by management.

If you want similar results for a team you lead—or a team you are in—start by embracing a culture of respect, social sensitivity, and the idea that it's everyone's responsibility to co-create a psychologically safe environment.

THE HIDDEN WORKPLACE
DYNAMIC THAT IS KILLING
YOUR COMPANY'S INCLUSION

While psychological safety—in an environment that preserves face—is a crucial element in developing a team willing to think innovatively, it gets you only partway there. If your team has insiders and outsiders, you aren't cultivating a truly inclusive environment. A team is more than just a group of people—it's a combination of people bringing their individual talents to reach a shared objective and being valued for their contributions.

Diversity and inclusion aren't just trendy business buzzwords. Research suggests that companies that embrace diversity perform better than companies that don't make it a priority. And diversity represents more than just ethnicity—it's also about demographics, experiences, and culture.

Who are insiders and outsiders?

The terms "insider" and "outsider" might bring to mind popular teenagers who actively exclude others from joining their clique. But in the context of a corporate environment, the behaviors at play can be much more subtle, embedded, and even undetected.

Consider one of my clients, Noah, who works for an international technology company. Noah's team is composed of people in the same time zone as the corporate headquarters, while others, like Noah, live several time zones away. Noah often starts his day by working on a project, only to learn that the company changed direction or canceled the project completely the night before. He and his local colleagues were left out of the decision-making because they were asleep. Noah feels like an outsider, while the rest of his team are perceived as insiders.

Noah's experience was a result of structural challenges. But workplace culture can unintentionally create an insider/outsider dynamic, too. Gender, race, and religious differences can have significant impacts on group dynamics as well.

Workers who smoke might discuss business with other smokers during smoke breaks, leaving nonsmokers out of the loop. A company might schedule activities around drinking during its annual summit, making nondrinkers feel left out. A manager might simply respond more positively to people with outgoing personalities, elevating their voices and ignoring those who are more reserved.

What's the impact of an insider/outsider dynamic?

When an insider/outsider dynamic exists, it can cause unintended bias in decision-making and unconscious biases in the selection and grooming of individuals for promotion.

There can be excessive barriers based on hierarchy—those on the "outside" simply can't break through the barriers that would place them on the "inside."

This dynamic can also create unequal and inequitable standards. Simply said, the "insiders" can seem to operate with their own rules and norms, while the "outsiders" don't know what those are. Only when insider/outsider dynamics are shattered can leaders start to build toward a truly inclusive environment.

What can leaders do to break down the barriers?

The key to dismantling an insider/outsider dynamic is for leaders to be aware of when the dynamic is occurring and take immediate steps to override it: share information; include all invested parties in decision-making; share the unwritten rules with people who don't know them; elevate and empower people so they can break through the barriers of hierarchy.

Amplify voices that aren't being heard. Leaders who create cultures of innovation and trust find a way to make sure everyone feels involved, contributes, and senses their contributions are valued. "It's not about conforming and having everybody agree on everything," my client Darlene Solomon, chief technology officer of Agilent Technologies, says.[5] In fact, not everyone's idea will get a green light. But how you make those people feel about those contributions is key. "A leader is stronger by explaining why they made the decision they did," Solomon says. Just do so in a way that's inclusive and not divisive—for example, by telling someone that a suggestion that didn't make it actually helped the team realize and understand a greater point. The result is that person doesn't feel rejected—they feel valued and are likely to come forward with suggestions in the future.

Never say failure. "When a project ends, we review what we learned, what we might do differently if appropriate, or maybe how we're going to take those learnings in a new direction," Solomon says. One word that never comes up? Failure. "We don't call them failures per se. It's about, 'what do we do next?'" This culture neutralizes the fear of failure, which can paralyze creative thinking. "I don't think that failure is even part of our day-to-day vocabulary," Solomon says.

Innovation is not a hardwired, innate gift. It's not native to a particular region or nation. It flourishes in the right kind of environment, which any leader with sincere intent can create. "Innovation is all about challenging the status quo, and I believe that creative, motivated people generally have great ideas and innovate well," Solomon says. "And as leaders we need to provide the right culture and the right leadership to sustain that innovation."

Likewise, because innovation doesn't solely exist in one area, the type of environment that encourages innovation isn't one size fits all, either. The one constant is that, whatever shape it takes, an ideal environment for fostering innovation is one that preserves face so that members of a team have the confidence to branch out and explore new ideas.

The Language Barrier

My client, a global company headquartered in Japan, had one team of Japanese employees in the U.S. office who reported to an American manager. The Japanese employees would usually speak Japanese to each other. The American team members assumed that they were talking about them or making decisions without their input or involvement. When confronted about this, the Japanese team said, "No, that is not the case at all. We speak Japanese to each other because our English is not good enough to understand the entire issue. So we speak to each other in our

native language to help each other understand the complex issue, clarify the language confusion, and summarize it for each
other, so we can all be on the same page. The Americans are
making wrong assumptions because of our language barrier!!"

THE SOLUTION: *Once we understood the situation,*
we developed a process for team meetings in which the
team leader would leave sufficient time for the Japanese
group to talk to one another in Japanese. Then the whole
group would reconvene to discuss solutions and make
decisions together.

People have a natural inclination to gravitate toward
things that they know. When working with a diverse group
of people, a leader needs to understand this and create an
environment that allows people to work in their comfort zone
but also structure it in a way that is inclusive of everyone. Of
course, it becomes that much easier to save face when you're
operating in a space where uncertainty and the feeling that
you don't know what's going on are minimized.

Simple tips in everyday communication can foster an
environment of trust and inclusiveness. Take the following
technique from Pixar.

Pixar's Plussing Technique

Pixar Animation Studios has encouraged an
environment for all of their creators and staff where
they look at all ideas or comments as a positive step in
the right direction. They call it a "Plussing" technique.[6]

When potential ideas or storylines are brought up by someone,
instead of responding with a "Yes, but . . ." comment, they start
with "Yes, and . . ." They use nonjudgmental language and do
their best to build on others' ideas.

On the surface, you might not think that changing one conjunction to another would transform a work environment to one that encourages risk-taking and innovation. And you'd be right. But when it comes to psychological safety, inclusiveness, and, of course, face, it's less about the words you use and more about what you mean authentically.

You might ask, "What is all this about innovation and mindfulness? I thought this book was about saving face." You're absolutely right. This book is all about saving face. But maybe the better question to ask is "What happens when you do save face?"

The answer, especially if you've managed to ingrain the importance of saving face into your team's DNA, is that many of the challenges that organizations face on a day-to-day basis—miscommunication, office politics, working in silos—all fall away when people feel valued and are rewarded for stepping outside their comfort zones. And the fruit of your efforts? A team working together, with an innovative mindset. That's the payoff.

CHAPTER 6

How to **BUILD**
Relationships
Using Face

'VE NEVER UNDERSTOOD "Open House" for-sale signs. Don't get me wrong. I've gone to open houses for many reasons—to get design ideas for remodeling our own home, to get a better idea of the neighborhood and the type of homes in the area, or just out of pure curiosity. Of course, I've also gone to open houses when I'm in the market for a new home. But curiously enough, as I suspect with most people, I've never bought a home after passing an "Open House" sign and deciding to turn in and have a look. If you think about it, though, maybe it's not that curious.

It's one thing if you are on a real estate search site, actively looking for a three-bedroom townhouse with a small yard close to your school of choice, and find such a home that happens to have an open house coming up. But for me, passing an "Open House" sign on a street corner is basically the real estate agent saying, "Come take a look at a random house you know nothing about, on the off chance that it's exactly what you're looking for." It's not exactly the most targeted approach to selling your home.

Now consider what an architect does for a client.

If you hired an architect to design your dream home, what would be the first thing to happen? The architect would schedule a sit-down with you and ask you hundreds of questions to better understand the requirements you have for your new home. You might not even know exactly what you want, but it's the architect's job to probe and lead you to develop some solid ideas of the kind of house you'd like to live in. Do you want to live in a ranch or two-story home? Do you want to have a retreat in the master bedroom or save that space for larger walk-in closets? Do you want the master bedroom on the first floor or on the second? The options are endless. It makes no sense for the architect to do it any other way. Having the architect dream up his vision of your perfect house without knowing exactly what you need is a waste of time for both of you.

The same principle applies to developing business relationships. Too many people approach the situation like the "Open House" sign—just open up for business, wing it, and see what shakes out. They treat their business as though they were a handyman. They have definite skills, but they go into a situation and see what is going on before they come up with a solution. While that might be fine for a handyman, it doesn't work when building a house or when establishing business relationships.

A person selling their home with this approach is only losing their time and effort. With business relationships, you could very well damage or actually lose a relationship with a critical partner. The stakes are much higher.

Here is where we get to the crux of what I do with all business leaders. If you believe it's important to save face when working with people locally or across the globe, you must be an architect. You must be a builder. You're the architect of every relationship you need to develop, and the builder of every achievement that relationship fulfills. As always, saving

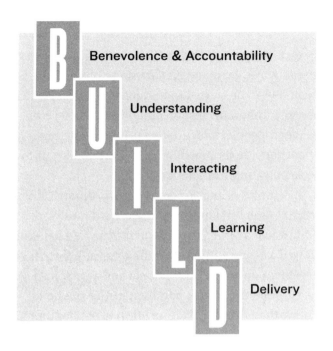

Benevolence & Accountability

Understanding

Interacting

Learning

Delivery

or preserving face is the key, and as a business architect, I've found that these five keys are crucial building blocks to forming strong, productive business relationships. It's what I call the BUILD model.

If the last chapter was about creating the best environment or, to make another analogy, setting the table, this chapter, with these five elements, is where we start to eat!

 Benevolence and Accountability

About thirty-five years ago, my late father-in-law, Dr. Shu-Yun Chan, pooled every last dollar he had and mortgaged his home to buy a small hotel in downtown San Diego. He had never owned or run a hotel before, but after decades of work as an electrical engineering professor, he wanted to fulfill his lifelong ambition of running his own business.

It was a struggle at first, and, as any first-time business owner can attest, he made his fair share of mistakes. But after the first year, he started to find his way. He knew that one of the most important responsibilities as a hotel owner was to hire good people, which is what he did. He hired a general manager, a hotel manager, and a group of staff to cover housecleaning and front desk duties.

As an employer and a person, a few things came naturally to my father-in-law. He worked hard and worked long hours. But just as important, he demonstrated benevolence: he showed a sincere interest in the lives of his staff, getting to know them on both a professional and a personal level. He would surprise them with bonuses during the holidays, but even more than that, he made an effort to support them, even in things that had absolutely nothing to do with their work.

If an hourly employee needed to go to the dentist and didn't have the money, somehow the bill would get covered. If another employee got in a car accident and the insurance didn't completely cover everything, my father-in-law would step in to make up the difference. It wasn't just the big things, either—he took the time to get to know his staff and show that he cared. Thirty-five years later, most of the hotel staff is still working at the hotel. And even more telling, my father-in-law passed away ten years ago. It just goes to show that even the smallest kindnesses can leave long-lasting impressions.

And this leads us to accountability. I grouped "benevolence" and "accountability" together specifically, because without accountability, benevolence might leave the impression that lasting business or personal relationships depend on never challenging or correcting behavior in order to maintain harmony, which obviously doesn't work.

After all, my father-in-law didn't engender the loyalty of his hotel staff by simply ignoring mistakes or issues that affected the business. It's not about simply "going along to get along." It's about addressing issues and problems in a benevolent way. Whether my father-in-law knew it or not, what he was doing by supporting his staff was practicing benevolence. In business as in life, it's an essential aspect of developing strong and durable relationships. Benevolence is defined as "any kind act, but can also be described as the desire to do nice things." But benevolence in the context of global leadership is much more than just doing "nice things," particularly when dealing with colleagues or peers across the globe.

In many parts of Asia, Confucianism has played an important role in the dynamics of both personal and professional social interactions. Many people in this region of the world subscribe to Confucius's teachings of "Five Basic Relationships." According to Confucius, every member of society fits into one or more of the five basic relationships, which are:

> Ruler and Subject
>
> Father and Son
>
> Elder and Younger
>
> Husband and Wife
>
> Friend and Friend

Confucius described how, in all but the last of these, the relationships involved the authority of one person over another. This meant that, for example, a son must obey, respect, and defer to his father, and the same with subjects and their ruler. However, balancing that deference, the person in the "superior" position has the responsibility of caring for and supporting their subordinate.

Now take that framework and apply it to today's workplace. In the relationship between a manager and employee, employees naturally defer to and obey the instructions of their manager. However, the responsibility to support and nurture their subordinates isn't taken nearly enough by managers. Without a manager's benevolence toward their direct reports, it's hard to develop a team with any sense of loyalty. If the relationship between manager and direct report or peer-to-peer is primarily a transactional one, meaning that they work together only to serve their own needs and not anyone else's, there is very little cohesiveness. This helps explain why many global companies often deal with high employee turnover in the Asia Pacific region.

I recently coached a global executive (whom we'll call Peter) based in North Carolina. Much of his team was based in Beijing. I was asked to do a 360-degree feedback assessment of his leadership skills by interviewing his boss, direct reports, peers, and coworkers. Some of them are in Beijing and some in the United States. In my interaction with Peter, I found him to be conscientious, kind, and well equipped to do his job. Unfortunately, the assessment of his leadership skills was just the opposite.

Here are some of the comments in his report.

- He parachutes in every few months and just starts asking us questions, demanding reports and updates. He doesn't really understand what we have to deal with on a day-to-day basis.

- He's very cold. He sets up in one of our offices and summons us one by one to report to him.

- He's not approachable.

- He is impatient and always in a hurry. When I presented business updates at staff meetings, he would say, "Got it. Got it." But I was not finished. He made me look bad in front of other colleagues.

- If a mistake was made by the staff, he'd point out the person(s) responsible for it at the team conference call. It made everyone feel uncomfortable.

After going through his assessment, I asked Peter to give me some perspective on how he manages his team.

He said, "There's so much to be done, so when I go to Beijing every three months, I do my best just to get up to speed as quickly as possible and make sure everything is on track. Then, when all the meetings and updates are complete, I go back to North Carolina and make sure the rest of the team is focused on their objectives."

After I spent some time with Peter, we talked about the need to reach out to his team in other ways, beyond just doing the tasks at hand. We talked about ways he could practice benevolence to build rapport and trust and to take the time to better understand the actions of his team and the context. Based on these discussions, he made a few changes during his next trip.

The first thing he did was to collect all the birthdays of his direct reports. On the day of their birthday, he would write a simple email wishing them a happy birthday along with other personal thoughts.

He extended the number of days he would spend in Beijing in order to invest more time to get to know his team. He made an effort to have lunch or dinner with the team or with individual team members, and played Ping-Pong with his team and cross-functional peers during lunch breaks.

Instead of summoning team members into his office to sit across from him while he sat behind an executive desk, he moved two sofas and a coffee table into the office so they could sit in a more relaxed way. With each meeting, he would offer them tea and spend some time chatting about things unrelated to work.

When discussing work issues with them, he would take the time to ask for their perspective, listen without interrupting, and work with them to come up with solutions. Most importantly, he created a "no-blame" culture by focusing on building trust and fixing the problems at hand, rather than finger pointing.

Three months after making these changes, a follow-up feedback interview was done with his team, and the responses were remarkable. Some of the comments were:

- I've seen a huge change with Peter. He is such a nice boss!

- I feel very lucky to be working with him. I am more comfortable talking with him now. I feel like he is there to help me, especially if there are problems.

- I am surprised he remembered my birthday! It warms my heart.

Earlier I said that benevolence, when applied in a workplace setting, is much more than just about being nice. But don't get me wrong—it doesn't necessarily mean having to do something big or costly either. The key is to put some thought into it and, most important, be genuine. It could simply be having some pizzas delivered when your team has to work late. Even if you're half a world away from your team, the odds are that there's a local food delivery service close to them! Whatever you can do to practice benevolence, just do it. It's something they will appreciate and remember.

 Understanding

You might recall, back in the 1980s during the early years of David Letterman's *Late Night* talk show, a recurring segment on the show was called the "Late Night Monkey-Cam

Mobile Unit." The segment entailed a roller-skating monkey wearing a backpack with a fixed video camera sticking up over his head that filmed the monkey in all of its movements. The camera was a precursor to today's action camera units worn by athletes when they are skiing, biking, or hiking in the wilderness.

Letterman's audience would howl in laughter as they watched the video feed of the monkey roller-skating over ramps, swooping across the studio floor and up across Letterman's desk, and weaving around the studio cameras on the floor. What fascinated me back then, when I first saw it, was that the audience (and those of us at home watching it on TV) was both laughing as well as fascinated at the randomness of what the monkey was looking at—a quick sweep of the items on Letterman's desk, then a tilted view of a ladder off to the side of the studio set, then a long glance at the edge of one of the ramps.

It's not that we were seeing anything that we hadn't seen before—we've all seen the typical things you'd find on a desk, a ladder, or any of the number of things the monkey was looking at while he was rolling around. The difference in what we were seeing was the perspective. As silly as the segment was (and that was, of course, Letterman's intent), the change in perspective makes viewing fairly mundane objects seem almost foreign—everything looked different through a different lens.

To bring that back around to the second letter of our BUILD acronym, the ability for a leader to truly *understand* the dynamics within a business team requires the leader to view situations from different perspectives. In order to be able to save face for those on your team and get the clearest understanding of complex problems and obstacles, you as a leader must be able to view the situation from different angles.

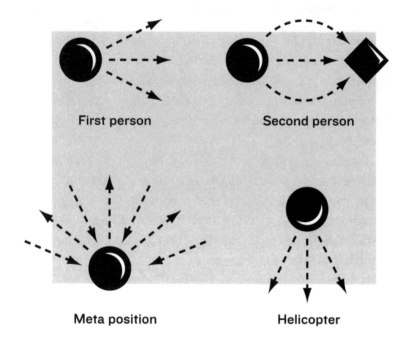

First person   Second person

Meta position   Helicopter

Leaders can view complex issues in a multicultural busi-ness environment from four different perspectives: first per-son, second person, meta position, and helicopter.

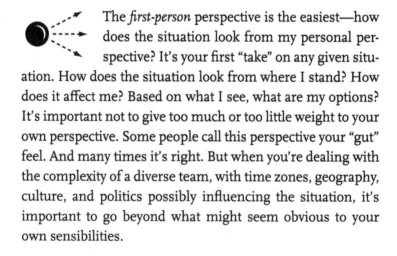

The *first-person* perspective is the easiest—how does the situation look from my personal per-spective? It's your first "take" on any given situ-ation. How does the situation look from where I stand? How does it affect me? Based on what I see, what are my options? It's important not to give too much or too little weight to your own perspective. Some people call this perspective your "gut" feel. And many times it's right. But when you're dealing with the complexity of a diverse team, with time zones, geography, culture, and politics possibly influencing the situation, it's important to go beyond what might seem obvious to your own sensibilities.

 The *second-person* perspective is the ability to put yourself in someone else's shoes. When looking at a complex problem or obstacle impacting other members of the team or a cross-functional colleague, try to put yourself in their position. How would you feel if you were "them"? Why do you think they behaved the way they did? What could have influenced their decision-making? By placing yourself in someone else's shoes, you free yourself from the restrictions of your own beliefs and standards and allow yourself to consider other possibilities, which can lead to a fuller picture of what might be going on.

 The *meta position* is in some ways both the easiest and the hardest position to occupy. In the meta position, your job is to be in the midst of the situation, soaking up everything and staying engaged. It's easy in that your main objective is to absorb all the information about a particular situation or problem. The hard part is that you need to set aside your own predilections, biases, and preferences to gain as much open awareness as possible. Ask yourself, Based on what I am observing, what can be my blind spots? What is happening that I'm not aware of? What hasn't been said? What advice would I give to all parties involved? By the time you've reached this third (meta) position, you are able to put together an assessment of the situation, even if you don't have every piece of the puzzle. But there's still one perspective left.

 The *helicopter* perspective allows a leader to step back and view the situation at hand from a distance—to see the forest instead of just the trees. By stepping back, you can see all the stakeholders interacting with one another and get a stronger sense of what is causing a problem, how it affects each stakeholder, and how to direct your efforts to tackle the issue in a thorough and holistic way.

A perfect example of this is a scene from the Tom Hanks movie *Cast Away*. Toward the beginning of the movie, Hanks's character wakes up after a tumultuous night of clinging to a life raft in the ocean during a monster storm and finds that he's landed on the beach of a tropical island. After collecting as much debris and other material to help him survive, he wanders along the length of the beach and into the jungle to determine where he is, or at least the nature of his situation. He doesn't know if he's on an island or at the edge of a larger territory, and he doesn't know whether there might be others nearby who might be able to help him. It isn't until he climbs up to and walks around the circumference of the highest peak on the island and sees nothing but ocean surrounding the tiny island that he discovers that he is truly alone, and realizes he will have to survive completely on his own.

There's a Chinese saying that simply translated says, "Don't be a frog living at the bottom of a well." Such a frog has a very narrow view of the world. All the frog can see is a tiny sphere of sky. Only by climbing (or leaping) out of a well can a frog really get a fuller perspective of the world. Like Hanks's character in *Cast Away* or a frog stuck in a well, a leader can't truly comprehend the depth of a problem or obstacle in a business dilemma if they aren't able to step back and view the situation in its entirety, with all the complexities that come from working with a group of diverse talents. Seeing the whole view allows the leader to come up with a systemic approach to any situation. Only by viewing the situation as a whole can you see how one decision will impact the decisions and options of others in the organization. Every complex organization is a web of communication between people working near and far—a global leader must see how every decision has an impact far beyond what they might normally expect.

The ability of a global leader to clearly understand situations that arise within a complex business environment, and come up with solutions that will address the situation directly and completely, ultimately keeps the team working productively and saves face even during a crisis.

 Interacting

I once had a Singaporean executive come to me, looking distraught. I asked him what was the matter. He said, "My boss thinks that I'm stupid. He thinks that I'm an idiot."

Having met his American boss, I immediately thought there must be some kind of mistake. I said, "Are you sure? What exactly did your boss say to you?"

He said, "I was giving him a report on an important project we've been working on. An issue came up and I needed to make a decision, which I did. So I reported back on what my decision was and I told him what I'd done. He said, 'Alright, that's a no-brainer.'"

I immediately explained to my client that his boss had no issues with his intelligence. What his boss was actually saying was that his decision made absolute sense.

The third letter in our BUILD model is "I," for "Interacting." In order to be an effective global leader, your skill set must include the ability to thoroughly interact with your boss, peers, direct reports, business partners, and customers, whether they are in your office or located thousands of miles away. To interact means far more than the ability to communicate verbally or electronically via email or text.

Studies show that when someone communicates, particularly when speaking or giving a presentation, only 7 percent of the message conveyed is the result of the actual words used. As much as 93 percent of the message is conveyed through body language, the tone and rhythm of the voice, and the pace and volume of the voice.[1]

In my earlier example of my client's reaction to his boss's "no-brainer" comment, much of that confusion was due to the boss's use of a colloquialism. Words certainly do matter. However, when working with any team, what you convey without uttering a word is at least as important as the words you do use.

Here's another example. You're working on a complicated project. You have a decision to make, but, no matter what you choose to do, some people will be happy and some will be irate. You text a colleague overseas and let her know what you've decided to do. After sending her the text, you receive a short reply: "Well, that's just great."

Was your colleague supportive or not? Did she take the news well or not? Without any context, these four words could have completely different meanings. She could be relieved that you made a terrific decision, or she could be reeling from all the extra work she now faces because of the awful choice you made.

Now take the same example but, instead of a text, imagine that you've walked over to your colleague in the office and told her your decision face-to-face. How much more likely are you to understand her response? Why? She might utter the same four words, but from just a few simple gestures—a smile, a stern look, hands clasped or covering her face—you'll know exactly where she stands. And in this situation, no one loses face because a message was misinterpreted.

As important as it is to be aware of both words and nonverbal cues, another aspect of interaction is crucial to developing a strong connection with those around you: building trust and establishing relationships. It sounds like common sense, but for some people, it's a huge challenge. But without having a strong connection with those you work with, the only thing you have to go on is what they say or do.

Think about it this way—interaction is the here and now. Communication, both verbal and nonverbal, is interpreted in and of itself because that's all you have to consider. When you've established rapport, or a strong connection with those on your team, the message conveyed by someone is informed by what you know of them—their desires, their preferences, their motives, and their personality. If you hear someone say, "I know that's what he said, but I know him, and that's not what he meant," you know the speaker can say that because they've established rapport.

You can see how developing an understanding with others is a fundamental part of developing a strong, cohesive global team. By understanding your colleagues' sensibilities, you can overcome many potential communication land mines; if someone says something completely out of character, you can first consider the possibility that they simply misspoke, or were using a term or phrase you simply weren't familiar with.

Beyond your capacity to communicate effectively, there's a side benefit to developing strong bonds with others on your team. Quite simply, building rapport makes you a better leader in the eyes of those you work with. Let me give you an example.

I was coaching a client not too long ago. On the surface, everything seemed to be going very smoothly. He was the top performer in a very established company, in a very competitive industry. His sales figures were always among the highest. He consistently beat his sales targets and his compensation was always in the highest tier. Yet he had been passed over for promotion several times. Although he achieved nearly all his performance goals, he couldn't seem to move up the corporate ladder.

As an executive coach, one of the first things I do when working with a new client is to do 360-degree stakeholder feedback interviews to get an understanding of how my coachee is perceived by those around him. During the interviews, I pose a series of questions to the coachee's peers, direct reports, and superiors to provide anonymous feedback on the overall performance of the coachee. The results in this instance were eye-opening.

He's not a team player.

He only talks to me when he needs something. He never offers to help others.

He behaves as if his success is through his efforts alone.

He's not collaborative.

When I reviewed these results with my client, he was nearly in tears. He felt that he was misunderstood. He had made a commitment to be the best salesperson he could be and would often spend late nights at the office making phone calls or putting together support materials for a potential customer. In fact, he appreciated all of the people he worked with, but he had just never made any time to get to know them and show his appreciation.

As I told him, it doesn't matter how many accomplishments you have if those around you don't like you or trust you. We brainstormed and came up with a few simple steps for him to take. At the end of each day, he was to reflect on the events of the day, ask himself, "Whom should I thank?," and write a note to express his sincere appreciation and gratitude.

Other steps included "Proactively reach out to peers to offer your help. Greet people when you see them and show your interest." The key was to be genuine and be consistent.

Establishing rapport takes more than showing people that you are an interesting person. It's much more important to show that you are interested in them. Being interesting lasts a few minutes. Being interested creates ongoing rapport.

Six months after our meeting, our follow-up 360-degree report came in, and the results were telling:

> He is like a different person now. He's warm and helpful.

> He's made a great effort to connect. He's much easier to work with lately.

> I look forward to working with him. He inspires us to do our best.

Interaction involves both the message and the method of conveying the message. It's also about creating the context in which clear conversations can be had. And of course, the ability to interact effectively creates an environment where "face" is protected and strengthened.

 Learning

The fourth letter of our BUILD model is the letter "L," which stands for learning.

Bill Gates, founder of Microsoft and one of the wealthiest men on earth, recently revealed that one of his biggest regrets was not learning a second language. During a Reddit chat, he said, "I feel pretty stupid that I don't know any foreign languages."[2]

Think about it. This man created a company that produces

software used by more than 90 percent of computer users. And if that weren't enough, he may have the most notable second act of anyone in history. The Bill and Melinda Gates Foundation is the largest charitable foundation in the world and is rapidly working to cure many of the globe's greatest ills—poverty, water sanitation, and malaria, among others. Even with all of those accomplishments, there's more that he would like to learn.

It just goes to show that the most successful people on earth, and its greatest leaders, have a constant urge to learn new things. They know that, in the grander scheme of things, their personal knowledge base is minute, and the rapid change of the world demands that they make the effort to stay current. They manage to keep the curiosity of youth throughout their adult years.

I tell my clients that there are four "P's" when it comes to learning:[3] passion, practice, persistence, and pattern recognition. Let me go through them quickly.

Passion is almost self-explanatory, indicating someone's motivation to learn. Unless you can muster the passion to learn something new, you probably won't.

Practice is also obvious—as the saying goes, "Practice makes perfect." In Malcolm Gladwell's best seller *Outliers*, he explains how the genius of the Beatles was due not only to the collective brilliance of John, Paul, George, and Ringo, but also, to a great degree, to the thousands of hours they spent in their early days playing in seedy clubs in Hamburg, Germany.[4] They spent countless nights working long hours at small gigs to earn a living, but more important, they spent their days practicing and refining their craft. That practice gave their inherent gifts a way to blossom that changed the musical landscape forever.

Persistence is the third "P," and persistence is what pushes people to go beyond what they think they can do. Persistence is what makes people look at the equation one more time, or do the extra push-up, or rewrite that crucial report. As the saying goes, "If it were easy, everyone would do it." It's the persistent ones who manage to accomplish the hard things.

Once you've mastered the first three "P's," passion, practice, and persistence, your efforts will inevitably lead you to the fourth "P," **pattern recognition**. Pattern recognition occurs when you've begun to master a particular skill or subject and you've learned enough to spot patterns or trends that others don't see. You become stronger in your skills and the task at hand becomes easier.

 Delivery

Delivery is where the BUILD model all comes together. You've demonstrated to your team that you practice benevolence and accountability. Those on your team, through your actions, can see that you have their best interests at heart. You've made an effort to understand the dynamics of your team both locally and globally. You've looked at the team from different angles—face-to-face and from afar. You interact with your team on a regular basis, getting to know their interests and their personal and professional goals, and show a general interest in them. And you push yourself to learn more about the functions of your job, of the team at large, and what the company is setting out to do. Delivery is simply putting it all together.

While the BUILD model will certainly benefit leaders working in any capacity, it's particularly relevant for global leaders working cross-culturally because it gives them the tools necessary to overcome differences in language, culture, time zones, politics, and geography. It's a powerful combination. The BUILD model is the key to being a powerful leader. It puts strong teams on a solid footing and it can turn around teams that succumb to office politics or overall dysfunction. Your team can become a symphony, working in harmony and in unison.

Now let's look at what to do when life or business throws you a curve.

CURVE BALLS

Successful leaders face curve balls on a daily basis. Curve balls are unexpected situations that might at first seem inexplicable. If used correctly, the BUILD model can help break through such situations and lead to better outcomes. Let's look at an example.

> *I know of a senior executive at Caterpillar Inc., which produces engines, construction machinery, and other services all over the world. This executive, whom we'll call Larry, was based in Thailand but had been born and raised in the United States; he was working to establish Caterpillar's products in Thailand. One of his clients, an industrial supplier, had been selling a large number of Caterpillar's engines. After a number of meetings with Larry, they began discussing the possibility of creating a rental program so that their customers would have access to Caterpillar's engines without necessarily having to buy one.*
>
> Following the BUILD model, Larry followed all the right steps. He met repeatedly with his main contact at the supplier, in formal meetings as well as social settings, to establish a relationship based on trust and friendship (Benevolence). He spent time

learning about the supplier's business and what their customers' needs were (Learning). Based on what he learned, he was the first to come up with the novel idea of an engine rental business, which seemed to meet the needs of the supplier's customers. To further flesh out the rental business concept, he decided, along with his main client contact, to present the rental idea to his contact's senior vice president and, if that went well, to the president of the company.

After the meeting, where they shared the idea of renting Caterpillar's engines to their customers for short-term use, the senior V.P. was even more enthusiastic about the idea and felt it was exactly what the company needed. He suggested that they jointly present the idea to the company president and offered some tips to Larry for his presentation that would likely help make his case.

The next week, Larry and the two managers sat down to meet with the company president. Larry proceeded to make his case to the president, using some of the tips the senior V.P. had given him, and he thought he was making a compelling case as to why the rental engine business could be a big boon for the supplier.

After listening intently to Larry's presentation, the president of the company quietly turned to his two managers and, speaking in Thai, quietly muttered a few sentences to them. Larry, who didn't speak Thai, waited patiently to get some reaction from the president. The president then turned to Larry, and, speaking calmly but deliberately, began to bring up a few reasons he didn't think the rental business would work. Larry jotted down the president's reservations; while the issues were relevant, Larry felt that each issue could be fairly easily addressed.

But before Larry could address the president's issues, his main contact and the senior V.P. immediately began echoing the president's concerns; they even came up with other obstacles that would keep a rental business from succeeding. They continued to voice their concerns and seemed determined to back up everything their president had just said.

Larry sat silent for a moment, but his immediate internal reaction was powerful: *These two guys have no backbone! Are they so afraid of their boss that they'll cave at the slightest bit of disagreement? Do they ever stand up for anything? How can I trust anything that comes out of their mouths?*

Instead of voicing any irritation or frustration, Larry immediately set aside his first impressions of the situation and decided to step back and regroup. He knew, out of experience, that there must be something more to this story. He calmly asked the president if he could take some time to address his concerns and get back to him. The two executives seemed to voice their support for the idea, and the president readily agreed to the suggestion.

After the meeting, Larry and his two contacts walked to another conference room to debrief. Larry, without sounding accusatory or irritated, simply began asking questions of the two executives to get their input on how the meeting had gone. After some discussion, Larry was surprised to find out that the two executives actually thought the meeting had gone relatively well. They explained that their abrupt switch of position was simply out of deference to the president, so as not to create conflict that would cause anyone to lose face in the process. The president had mentioned in his brief aside to his two managers that he had put together a rental program for another product years ago, and the experience was both painful and unsuccessful. The two executives knew that trying to dissuade him right then would have been difficult, if not impossible.

Larry went back to his office and spent the next few days working out solutions to the president's concerns. A few days later, he first reached out to the two executives to share his solutions, got additional feedback from them, and, after incorporating their input into his presentation, he scheduled a follow-up meeting with the president and the two executives.

Larry began the presentation by acknowledging the president's concerns and welcoming his feedback, because the success of any rental program was just as important to him as it was for the president. He then began to tackle each issue head-on, with solutions that seemed to address the president's concerns.

This time, the president smiled, thanked Larry for his presentation, and then turned to the two executives and directed them to start putting plans together for the rental program. Many years later, the rental engine business for the supplier is the second-largest revenue generator for Caterpillar.

This experience really shows how the BUILD model can help a global leader tackle a multicultural challenge. Larry didn't give in to his first impulse—the idea that these two managers had no backbone and therefore couldn't be depended on. Instead, Larry took it upon himself to increase his interaction with the two executives and better understand the overall situation. He kept his cool and maintained a positive relationship with the two executives (Benevolence). He made the effort to determine what the real issues were between the two executives and the president (Understanding). He kept checking back with the executives to get their input before he followed up with the president (Interaction), and he took the time to truly see what the obstacles were so that he could come up with suitable solutions (Learning). And most important, he put everything together before his second meeting with the president (Delivery).

Because every situation is unique, a leader needs to know that the BUILD method is a continuous, persistent tool to be used. It's not a task that can be checked off and forgotten. It's one that needs to be used, and used again and again, until problems are truly identified and solutions are put in place.

This example also identifies one of many issues that, if not properly dealt with using the BUILD model, can derail even the best-laid plans. In this case, the abrupt shift in the behavior of the two executives when their president voiced his concerns could easily be viewed in two very different ways, depending on your culture. In Western culture, the perception would be that these two executives were weak, not having a mind of their own, and unable to stand up for what they believed in. From an Asian cultural perspective, however, the two executives were simply respecting their superior by showing deference; they knew that that particular moment was not the time to "close the deal" but was a time to regroup and plan for the next step. Along with showing benevolence, Larry took the time to understand and address the executives' perspective and why they had made a sudden turn away from the proposal, which is part of accountability. His constant application of the BUILD model allowed for the follow-up meeting that led to the business deal.

In this case, the BUILD model uncovered the propensity for Asian executives to "save face" in order to address an issue at a later date. The Asian culture's preference to avoid conflict, as well as varied perspectives on risk, initiative, and accountability, are just some of the challenges that global leaders must face every day, and it's important to recognize many of these factors as they arise. But first, let's try putting all of this in context.

On rare occasions, it's certainly possible that the BUILD model just isn't necessary. Theoretically, it's possible to consider a team where all relevant information is shared completely among all members. It's possible that the team has been together so long and has been involved together so thoroughly that any action taken by any one member is completely understood and correctly perceived. I suppose it's also possible that this team could be working with a group of clients and they, in turn, would also be on the same page with the team, with everyone working together without any conflicts or challenges whatsoever, because everyone understands the motivations and objectives of everyone else. While such a situation might exist somewhere out there in the real world, nothing is ever quite that pat or easy. In even the best of scenarios, team members move on, projects change, cultural issues are a constant influence, and challenges arise.

THE JOHARI WINDOW

The Johari Window was created by two American psychologists, Harrington Ingham and Joseph Luft.[5] The original intent of the Johari Window was to help people in their relationships with each other. Without going into too much detail (since you can google it just as well as I can!), the concepts involved with the Johari Window very helpfully highlight some of the challenges that leaders face on a regular basis. The basic concept of the Johari Window is that, that for any given issue, there are things that you know and don't know, as well as things that others know or don't know. The many combinations of these states cause potential conflict and confusion for leaders and their teams.

The BUILD model creates an environment and a process that overcomes the kinds of conflicts that arise and that often, as I'll show in the following example, are due to the loss, or potential loss, of face.

One of my clients, a major furniture manufacturer in North Carolina, asked me to figure out what their management needed to do in order to identify problems

*with their manufacturing partners in China. The
company had designed a new line of occasional tables
and they hired a furniture factory in Dongguan,
China, to manufacture them.*

The U.S. furniture company and the Chinese factory had worked
successfully together on various furniture designs, but this time
there were problems. The American company had sent detailed
blueprints for a set of occasional tables to the factory. As they had
in the past, the company worked out a timeline with the factory,
but as the deadline neared for initial samples of the tables, the
factory kept saying they needed more time. Another deadline
would be set, and sure enough, there would be another delay.

After several weeks of delays, and with a major furniture
show on the calendar forcing the issue, the American company
flew representatives out to the factory in Dongguan to see what
progress had been made on these tables as well as on a number
of other items.

In the factory's display area, the U.S. team was directed toward several samples of the tables. The tabletops and the legs
had the dramatic, wood-carved detail specified in the blueprints,
which made for a very romantic look. But there was one obvious problem. Halfway down each table leg was a shiny metal
rod connecting one leg to another, going all the way around the
table, almost like a footrest. The contrast between the curved,
sweeping, intricately carved wood and the smooth metal rods
between the legs was jarring. The two elements didn't match at
all. But most important, the bars were not part of the blueprint
design.

After a moment, the U.S. team leader looked up at the factory manager and asked, "Why did you put the bars on the table
legs?"

The factory manager said, "It's an improvement."

The U.S. team members looked at each other in puzzlement. After a moment, the team leader said, "Actually, we'd just like you to follow the blueprints as we've developed them. Just make the tables based on our design."

After completing all their business, the American team went back home. For the next few weeks, very little progress was made. Both sides met via videoconference, but the Americans could clearly see that, while some changes had been made, the metal rods were still there. When they pushed the factory manager to follow the designs exactly, the manager would jot down some notes and gently nod his head. Yet at the next meeting, the metal rods would still be there.

The U.S. team, meeting among themselves, was at a loss to understand what was going on. Did the Chinese factory team really think the metal rods were an improvement? Were they being defiant or completely incompetent? Why wouldn't they just follow the blueprints?

When I met with the U.S. team and they updated me on the situation, I also couldn't explain why the Chinese team was responding the way they were, but I was certain that there was a disconnect between the two teams that needed to be addressed.

I recommended that the American furniture company assign one of their employees, a local manager working in logistics but based in Dongguan, to set up shop in the Chinese factory and make himself available both to provide guidance and to better understand the situation. While the local manager didn't have much experience in furniture, he was local and could converse with the factory regularly.

Within a couple of days, their local manager contacted the U.S. team—he had the answer. He told the Americans that the reason the factory kept the metal rods in place was because the connection between the legs and the tabletop as laid out in the blueprints was unlike their normal designs; it included some metal joints that they had never used before and did not know how to source. The Chinese factory hadn't immediately disclosed this information because they felt it would be a loss of face to admit that they could not come up with a solution.

Once the problem was understood, the U.S. team leader assured the Chinese factory that the American company had the utmost confidence in them and wanted to work with them to come up with a solution. In the end, the teams worked together to find a supplier for the type of metal joints needed, and the tables were produced exactly in accordance with the blueprints.

This example clearly illustrates the complexity of social dynamics involved with global leadership and what can happen when some issues are unknown to one side or the other. The U.S. team knew what they wanted for the design of the furniture, they knew how it should be built, and they knew that they had worked successfully with the Chinese factory in the past. But they also knew that, for some reason, the factory in Dongguan was not coming up with an acceptable product.

The unknown factor—that the Chinese factory was unfamiliar with a crucial part of the product design but, to avoid losing face, was hesitant to admit it to their American partners—caused the U.S. team to have the inaccurate perception that their Chinese partners were either stubborn or completely incompetent. But by using the BUILD method, particularly the Understanding, Interacting, and Learning aspects of it, the U.S. team realized that the problem wasn't stubbornness or incompetence, but the importance of saving face.

You'd be surprised at how often leaders will come across very similar scenarios. Understanding that the need to preserve face is one thing. How a global leader discovers where and how to do so is key.

CHAPTER 7

Relearning
How to Drive

THINK ABOUT your daily commute to work. Not much to think about, right? If you're like me, you start the car and, the next thing you know, you're in the parking lot ready to tackle another day. Of course, you need to be careful whenever you're driving. But other than that, you know every street, every street sign, every mailbox, and every Starbucks along the way. There's really not that much effort involved in driving to work. You are literally on autopilot.

Now think about the last time you had to drive to an unfamiliar destination. Maybe you looked up the directions before you got in the car. Maybe you were fortunate enough to have a GPS system ready to help you get to your destination. Either way, I'll bet you had to take extra time to double-check every street sign, look out for the gas station on the corner that you were supposed to turn at, and check every address on the last block to make sure you found the right building. Even though driving on unfamiliar streets can be a challenge, it's still nothing you can't handle. You know how to drive, and, as long as you're paying attention, chances are very good that you'll reach your destination safe and sound.

Let's try one more.

Have you ever tried driving in another country where all the cars are driving on the opposite side of the road and the driver's seat has shifted to the other side as well? Mechanically, everything is exactly the same—the same four tires with the same engine and the same turn signals. Everything that should be there is there, but everything is fundamentally different. Instead of crossing over oncoming traffic to take a left turn, now you do it when making a right turn. Instead of passing cars on the left, now you do it on the right. You're operating a car essentially the same way you would during your normal commute to work, but if you go on autopilot this time, you could crash and burn.

Working cross-culturally is a lot like driving in a foreign country for the first time. Go on autopilot too quickly and you can easily crash and burn, too. Your driving skills, or in this case, your leadership abilities, skills that you've honed and refined over the course of your career and that have led to enormously successful ventures at home, can actually be a hindrance or a complete disaster if used in certain situations overseas. As it turns out, some commonsense business practices aren't so common once you've crossed international borders.

In my twenty-plus years of coaching executives of Fortune 500 companies, I've run into the same scenario time and time again. A successful executive (we'll call him John) who is a client of mine is charged with expanding his corporation's business overseas. John identifies a potential vendor abroad, and determines that this company has the resources and experience that his company is looking for. After a rush of meetings, contracts are signed and the new partnership begins in earnest. As with every other successful project John has ever worked on in his company, objectives are laid out and strict deadlines set for the new vendor. Everything is set to go.

Except that it doesn't. Some items get finished, but many are not. Some of the objectives are complete but not appropriately so. Seeing things are not going well, John starts to pressure his new partner, telling them that they have to live up to their agreement and threatening to pull out if they don't get their act together. John soon finds out that upping the pressure only seems to make matters worse. They fall farther behind. John, a perennial success at his company, went into autopilot with this new venture because that's what worked before. He never noticed he was driving on the wrong side of the road.

THE CULTURAL ICEBERG:
HOW WE PERCEIVE AND INTERPRET
EACH OTHER THROUGH AN INVISIBLE LENS

Picture yourself at your local McDonald's. You walk past the golden arches and into the store. Everything is immediately familiar to you—the tiled floors, the customers in line at the counter, even the straws and condiments on one side of the room. You step in line, look at the menu board, and . . . something is different.

Yes, you see a Filet-O-Fish, but there's no Big Mac. Not even a Quarter Pounder! Instead, you see the McDonald's staff dropping chicken patties into wax-paper bags filled with spices. The customer next to you orders a bowl of rice porridge topped with bits of meat, ginger, and chili peppers. Another customer orders an English muffin with Vegemite spread on top. Despite your bewilderment, you order a Filet-O-Fish and an apple turnover. But lo and behold, the one you ordered is filled with . . . taro?

Don't worry—you haven't stepped into the Twilight Zone.

Each one of the meals listed above is actually sold at McDonald's—overseas.

You might ask, why would McDonald's want to mess with a proven formula? The answer, of course, has everything to do with each country's unique culture and customs. McDonald's realizes that, while many aspects of the McDonald's experience work just fine universally, many of the foods being served need to accommodate each country's customers and their cultural uniqueness. That's why, instead of serving McDonald's hamburgers in India, their veggie burger is the hot item there.

For companies working around the globe, culture goes far deeper than that—literally. Think of every culture as being like an iceberg. The most visible part of an iceberg is, of course, the tip. What you perceive about people from other cultures—the way they speak, their mannerisms, their body language, all that is immediately visible—is just the tip of the iceberg. Remember that the bulk of any iceberg is submerged.

That's how culture works as well. The visual cues you perceive when you communicate with someone from another culture are readily apparent. What isn't obvious is the backstory behind those behaviors. The motivation, traditions, history, and religious beliefs of a culture that ultimately inform someone's behavior aren't immediately obvious. All of these influencers lie beneath the surface. They are 90 percent of one's cultural iceberg.

Let's try an example.

You're in a conference with managers from a factory in Dongguan, China. Your company has signed a contract with this factory to manufacture a revolutionary medical device that will ultimately save doctors and hospitals time and money. After exchanging pleasantries, you work your way through the agenda by asking various divisions of your company to make presentations. First, an engineering manager shares new production specifications that the factory managers need to adopt. Then a marketing manager from your team shares the results of the latest focus group findings. Finally, your accounting manager proposes that the factory managers add additional vendors to source some of the components used for the new product in order to get more competitive pricing.

During each presentation, the meeting seems to be going well except for one thing—no matter what you or your managers say, the factory managers just won't look you in the eye. Your first reaction is, what are they hiding from you? It's a natural response. If all the managers avert their eyes and generally avoid making eye contact, you think something must be amiss. They are not telling you something.

The problem with this reaction is that when someone from the West assumes that anyone who avoids eye contact must be hiding something, their perception is based on their own predilections, customs, and understandings. That is the submerged part of their cultural iceberg.

However, many people in Asia believe that to avert one's eyes is a show of respect. In their understanding, continuously looking into someone's eyes could be perceived as being too aggressive and disrespectful. Misunderstandings often occur when one person perceives someone else's behavior based on their own cultural iceberg.

Let's go back to the meeting. After your managers have finished their presentations, the factory managers barely utter a word and don't seem to have any questions, even after you've offered to answer any questions they might have. In fact, each time you ask a yes or no question, they politely nod their heads and say, "Yes, yes . . ." Based on their reaction, you suppose that they completely understand and agree with everything you've explained to them, especially since they have had every opportunity to ask follow-up questions.

The natural Western response to silence from someone is to assume that silence equals comprehension and/or agreement. However, silence from an Asian point of view does not necessarily signal such a reaction. In fact, one of the most common reasons Asians remain silent is because they may not understand what you just said. They don't want to lose face by admitting they don't understand. Another common reason is that they may *disagree* with you. They don't want to offend you or cause you to lose face, so they keep quiet. There are many potential reasons for silence, and agreement is probably not one of them!

THE HUMAN ANTENNA:
CULTURAL SENSITIVITY AND AWARENESS

Study the past, if you would divine the future.

—CONFUCIUS

The concept of saving or losing face is deeply rooted in the cultural icebergs that inform our behavior and personalities. But knowing and recognizing that everyone has a cultural iceberg is only the beginning. As any experienced seafarer in polar waters can tell you, a successful captain identifies icebergs in his path and sets out a plan to steer clear of them well in advance. The captain of a ship would rely on his sonar. But in cross-cultural business, we depend on what I call "the human antenna."

The human antenna is really nothing more than being sensitive to others when you are working with people from different backgrounds and adapting quickly to any situation. But how you calibrate that antenna makes a difference. Just as you would raise the antenna on a portable radio when you are trying to tune in to a weaker radio signal, global leaders need to raise their human antenna when working with diverse cultures, genders, generations, values, personalities, and other human differences.

Here's an example. Mark Jones, an executive from a major computer peripherals company in Atlanta, picked up an executive of a logistics company providing services to Mark's company, Molly Chiu, who arrived early in the morning on a flight from Asia. After he greeted her and loaded her luggage into the car, the two of them set off to a regional office for a round of meetings scheduled for the day. After a bit of small talk, Molly said, "You got up so early to pick me up, you must be hungry!"

Mark replied, "Oh, I'm an early bird and I had a big breakfast this morning. I'm good until lunch. Don't worry about me." Mark might want to have his antenna checked.

What Mark's antenna failed to pick up was that Molly was signaling that she was hungry, but would find it impolite to simply blurt out, "Can we go get something to eat first?" She didn't want to imply that Mark was not an attentive host and cause him to lose face.

The situation would be only marginally better if Mark had followed up his response with "Are you hungry?," since her likely response would be "It's okay. I don't want to make us late."

The proper response would have been something like, "Molly, you were on such a long flight. Let's stop off to get a quick bite to eat, since we have a long day ahead of us, okay?"

As we go through our day, each and every one of us uses a human antenna to help us interact with others. If you spend most of your day dealing with folks from the same cultural background—living and working in the same city, state, or even country—your human antenna is calibrated to deal with everyone you associate with every day. But for those who work cross-culturally, it's as though your human antenna picks up an AM signal while you're trying to tune into an FM channel—it just won't work.

What Mark, in the preceding example, failed to pick up was the difference between high- and low-context-oriented cultures. For people from low-context-oriented countries, such as the United States and the Netherlands, the primary purpose of communication is to convey information and opinions in a direct, straightforward way. In a business environment, low-context people have an objective at hand, and communication tends to be explicit, on point, and somewhat impersonal.

With high-context-oriented cultures, such as in Asia, communication is very contextual, based on past experiences, and very implicit in nature and tone. In a business environment with high-context-oriented communication, developing and strengthening relationships is at least as important as dealing with the business at hand. In fact, the success of the business is very often determined by the strength of the relationship between individuals and organizations.

With Molly and Mark, the misreading was due to a low-context-oriented person (Mark) missing the social cues of a high-context-oriented person (Molly). But make no mistake, such misreadings can go both ways.

Later in the day with Molly and Mark, Mark brought Molly to meet with his company's new V.P. of Operations, Jake Branson. Jake had asked Molly to develop some ideas to create efficiencies in their supply chain. In Molly's presentation, she proposed that, instead of warehousing all of their products at one large location in Dongguan, it would be more efficient to use smaller warehouses located near each of their manufacturing facilities throughout China, which would save overall transportation costs and time. After Molly finished her presentation, Jake smiled, thanked Molly for taking the time to put the proposal together, and said, "I'd like to think about it overnight."

Later that evening, Molly got back to her hotel and called her colleagues back in China. She said that the meeting with Jake had not gone well, and he seemed to have some problems either with the proposal or with her, and seemed hesitant about making any changes to the current system.

In this example, as a high-context-oriented person, Molly interpreted Jake's request to "think about it overnight" as a negative reaction, a possible response to not liking what he'd seen or possibly not liking Molly herself. But as a low-context-oriented person, Jake may have said that he wanted to "think about it overnight" because he just really wanted to "think about it overnight"! He may have simply wanted to spend some additional time thinking about his options.

Whether a culture is high or low context is largely influenced by its technological, political, sociological, and religious aspects. Technology specifically has rapidly expanded and accelerated the way people communicate on a daily basis, and it's changing our understanding of high- and low-context cultures.

Here in the West, more and more people find a smartphone to be an indispensable tool for organizing their lives, keeping track of information, and communicating. It's become a ubiquitous presence in our lives. And how do most folks communicate on their phone? They no longer use it as a telephone. They text, and they text a lot!

But here's where things get interesting. In the West, most people send short text messages back and forth throughout the day—the content of the messages tends to be short, like letting someone know that they'll be late, or a quick back and forth of how a meeting or party went.

As much as we see people walking around while staring at their phones, texting each other or posting on social media, this habit is even more prevalent overseas. In Taiwan, instead of regular texts, people tend to use a third-party texting service such as LINE, and it's much more social in tone. People share popular videos or information about a meal they had the night before, essentially using their texts as their social media.

In China, many people communicate using a third-party app called WeChat, and their texts have essentially replaced the use of email. Along with short texts about everyday activities, the Chinese will send out long, detailed articles and reports highlighting particular issues or events. Particularly the younger, or "Gen Y," generation will not only communicate but also conduct business through WeChat, using their texts as a primary form of communication. I've witnessed a Chinese doctor and his patient recording and sending detailed voice messages on WeChat back and forth to discuss the patient's diagnosis and transmit prescription information.

How this technology affects high- and low-context cultures is dramatic. In China, the older generation is still very much tied to high-context communication, where establishing relationships is paramount and what one says conveys far more meaning than the literal meaning of the words. But with the younger generation, the use of WeChat and other technologies inherently means that the network of people they communicate with expands beyond cities or even national borders; with less reliance on personal relationships or interactions, their communication styles are becoming less contextual and more direct.

As these variations demonstrate, cross-cultural communication is complex, and there isn't a monolithic culture in any country that allows a "one size fits all" technique for communication. That is why the human antenna and the ability to use it are essential for effective communication across cultures.

Just as a low-context-oriented person might miss social cues from a high-context-oriented person, a high-context-oriented person might pick up cues from a low-context-oriented person that simply aren't there. The key to both high- and low-context-oriented individuals communicating effectively with each other depends on their human antenna. Are they each able to set aside their cultural expectations and reinterpret social cues that are outside their normal communication paradigms? By developing skills to adapt to unfamiliar cultures instead of seeing them through one's personal prism, global leaders can communicate effectively with all cultures and see things as they were intended to be.

Culture in all its forms affects communication, understanding, and action. Without an effective way of managing cultural differences, misunderstandings and loss of face are almost inevitable. However, harnessing the diversity that comes with working across cultures uncovers resources and skills that can work to any organization's advantage. The next chapter looks at how a leader can embrace culture.

One of my favorite Chinese proverbs seems to fit this idea perfectly: 點石成金—*Turn stone into gold*—that is, work something of no worth into something of value.

CHAPTER 8

Cultural Agility

ET'S RECALL the Chinese saying "Don't be a frog living at the bottom of a well." The trapped frog has a very narrow view of the world. Only by leaping out of the well can he enjoy a fuller perspective.

The principles of saving face to preserve dignity and build trust are complicated enough within environments that we're accustomed to, where we speak the same language, have the same kind of life experiences, and have the same kind of expectations. But when you add cross-cultural issues—different languages, different upbringings, and diverse cultures—it becomes that much more of a challenge to apply the skills we've developed to preserve and save face. After all, how can you prevent someone from being humiliated if what you've done or said seems perfectly appropriate? This aspect of saving or preserving face within a diverse culture is something I call having *cultural agility*.

What is cultural agility? Simply put, it is the ability to look at a situation from a business and cultural perspective and manage it to achieve business results in a way that works effectively within the cultural context.

What is culture? According to Dutch psychologist Geert Hofstede, culture is "the collective programming of the mind that distinguishes the members of one group or category of people from others."[1] American anthropologist Edward T. Hall says, "Culture hides much more than it reveals, and strangely enough what it hides, it hides most effectively from its own participants."[2] Taken together, these definitions mean that culture is what makes every group unique, but it's also what makes all of us harder to understand.

If you consider the analogies of the cultural iceberg and the human antenna, and add the idea of relearning how to drive, you can see how these parts contribute to the whole of what it means to be an effective global leader. What do I mean? Let's take a look at how these analogies work together.

"Relearning how to drive" is really just shorthand to help a global leader recognize that for their company or team to go in a certain direction or achieve a particular goal in a cross-cultural environment, the path they take may not be one that they're used to. In fact, the way forward may seem completely counterintuitive to them. Forging a new path requires a global leader to have the self-awareness to know that what worked before might not work again in a global environment.

The challenge in moving forward on an unfamiliar path is understanding that what isn't known—the cultural iceberg—requires a global leader to consider how differences in culture, language, religion, and other factors could affect how a team or business works together. These factors are detours on the path to a successful team or business outcome. Cultural knowledge (or lack thereof) impacts how a team works together.

Finally, the human antenna represents the ability of a global leader to notice the subtle and not-so-subtle differences with cross-cultural teams in order to come up with a final roadmap for their team. It allows the global leader to integrate a style shift in order to adapt to differences in culture and behavior to move from a local mindset to a global one.

Self-awareness, cultural knowledge, and the ability to shift style—put these three elements together, and you have the makings of a successful global leader. That is the essence of having cultural agility.

Let me describe a perfect example of cultural agility at work. I don't have to look farther than my kid brother, Steven. He's not much of a kid anymore, but in a very immediate sense, he is the very definition of someone who is culturally agile. You see, my brother is a global tour guide. His business is to lead large groups of customers on tours throughout the world. His customers are primarily from Taiwan and China, and most of them don't speak a word of English (or French, or Spanish, or Hebrew . . . you get the idea). Every two weeks he takes a large group of tourists to the farthest reaches of the globe, and his sole objective is to make sure the trip is fun, educational, safe, and, most important, organized.

Within any given trip, Steven needs to navigate between the customs and culture of whatever country he's in and those of his clients. He needs to know both what food is available in whatever country he's in and also what his guests prefer. He needs to know whether his group would rather shop or visit a museum, and also needs to be aware that when they enter a cathedral in Italy, the women of his group must cover their shoulders with a scarf and the men must wear shorts that cover their knees.

There are very few countries he hasn't toured. Every country has its own customs, traditions, and standards, and Steven must navigate them all in conjunction with the preferences of whatever group he is leading at the time. Think about how many cultural pitfalls he comes across. How many people can he inadvertently offend? You might call what he does for a living "cultural agility on the fly."

Cultural agility for a global leader usually isn't as seemingly chaotic as one of Steven's trips, but the pitfalls can be just as precarious. Let me share another story, this one of a global leader who hasn't developed his cultural agility yet.

I was asked to coach a senior executive at a multinational telecommunication company—I'll call him Sam. Sam was considered a star of the company and had recently been promoted from a position where he worked entirely with a Chinese team to a higher-level position where he worked with Chinese, Japanese, and U.S. design teams. He had had very little experience in working with non-Chinese teams, and his English was not strong.

One of his main responsibilities was to run group conference calls between the three design teams to develop new tablet and computer models. In the past, when he was working with only the Chinese design team, the team, as was usual in Chinese culture, usually deferred to the senior manager, who was Sam. Basically, in their meetings, Sam would run the meetings, finalize design plans, and delegate responsibilities to members of his team.

But in this new global setting, Sam quickly realized that the dynamic had changed. Once objectives were set, members of the team, particularly the U.S. team, would outline their design ideas and persuade the rest of the team to go in their design direction. Sam was somewhat taken aback that the U.S. team had their own ideas and even asked for feedback from the other teams. Not knowing what to do, Sam would say, "That's fine," and the meeting would adjourn.

At this point, Sam would naturally revert back to the process that had worked in the past. He disregarded the ideas of the U.S. team and then met with his Chinese team to come up with a different solution; once that was completed, their design was sent to the U.S. team.

Understandably, the U.S. team expressed their frustration and confusion at having their own designs discarded and replaced with plans by the Chinese team without any input from the U.S. or Japanese teams. They wondered why Sam had said, "That's fine," if they were just going to change everything.

In this situation, Sam didn't have self-awareness. He was not aware that he was behaving from a very Chinese-centric position, where your ideas were discarded if a leader didn't know or trust you and ideas were favored based on the relationship he had with the local team. His style of leadership was hierarchical and relationship-based, not necessarily based on competence. Additionally, Sam's cultural knowledge was such that he was offended that the U.S. staff had other ideas than those of his Chinese team, and he was taken aback because he didn't understand that Western culture welcomes creativity, egalitarianism, and assertiveness.

Because Sam wasn't self-aware and didn't have enough cultural knowledge about the other teams he was working with, he couldn't shift his style. Instead of creating a very functional team, he created three teams pitted against one another. He was the center of his team and a big cause of their problems. In today's global economy, it's becoming imperative for more and more of us to be able to lead a group or a team cross-culturally. Being a global leader means having to be a perpetual style shifter.

THE **AAA** MODEL
FOR CULTURAL AGILITY

The most effective global leaders are style shifters with an uncanny ability to adapt to diverse people and climates. The AAA model (Aware → Acquire → Adapt) is a way for global leaders to put into practice a huge toolkit of concepts that at first may seem unnatural and counterintuitive to them.

The AAA Model

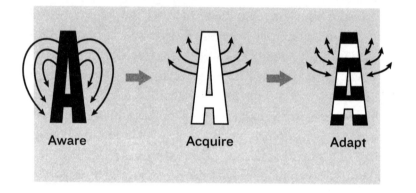

Aware   Acquire   Adapt

STEP I
Be AWARE of Your Own Culture
[*inward focus*]

- Know how your own culture and values shape your assumptions, thoughts, and behaviors.

- Know your own bias.

- Be comfortable with ambiguity.

- Manage your emotions.

- Be aware of your own actions and their impact.

- Talk openly about cultural differences and similarities.

STEP 2
ACQUIRE Cultural Knowledge
[*outward focus*]

- Learn as much as you can about the culture with which you are working.
- Develop a sense of curiosity.
- Cultivate a "learning mindset."
- Withhold judgment. Don't make assumptions.
- Listen to connect.
- Build a diverse network.
- Create engagement by finding commonalities.

STEP 3
ADAPT New Behaviors
[*bridging the difference*]

- Be open to different options.
- See each person as a unique individual.
- Accept and practice silence.
- Display empathy.
- Cultivate resilience.
- Be perceptive of subtle messages.
- Show respect to everyone.
- Avoid a "we" vs. "they" mentality.
- Switch styles when it is appropriate to do so.

Global leaders need candid self-*awareness* to know their own cultural values, assumptions, and even bias. They need to *acquire* knowledge of other cultures, understand and accept others' frame of reference, and grasp how social values, languages, religions, and many other factors could influence the way people work and communicate. Lastly, they must use their cultural antenna to detect the subtle and overt differences in diverse teams and *adapt* their behaviors to bridge the differences and develop creative solutions. The key elements of the AAA model are empathy and adaptability.

Let's look at an example of how cultural agility can be employed using the AAA method.

Tom is from the United States and has been working with a major multinational company for approximately six months. Raj is from India and has just started with the company. They are in the same team and report to the same manager, who is also from the United States.

While still fairly new himself, Tom has had some time to acclimate to the company culture and understand his manager's working style. Within the teams in the department, it is very common for employees with six to twelve months' experience to act as mentors to brand-new team members and provide assistance and guidance.

When Raj joins the team, Tom is happy to provide advice based on his experience as a new hire so far. He offers suggestions for new ways of doing things and possible tests to try. Based on their interactions, Tom feels everything is going well between him and Raj. A little time goes by and the manager calls Tom into her office for a meeting. The manager informs Tom that Raj came to see her to discuss the current team working situation. It comes as a surprise to Tom to learn that Raj has been uncomfortable with him providing suggestions and guidance for his work. Raj is very sensitive to company hierarchy and does not feel that someone who is not his manager should be telling him how to do things. Seeing Tom as a peer, he has been offended that Tom was giving him directions.

The manager tells Tom that she wants to be respectful of Raj's concerns, but she is comfortable with everyone's current role in the project. She tells Tom to be aware of Raj's sensitivities, and that in the future she may interact more with Raj on some of his responsibilities. She reassures Tom that any additional involvement from her is not a reflection on how he is handling things, but an effort to help Raj feel more at ease while he adjusts to the team's working style.

You see in this example that the manager worked with both Tom and Raj, understood each of their concerns (Aware), made each of them aware of the other's concerns (Acquire), and then deftly coordinated a process that could help both of them work better together (Adapt).

Of course, even the best preparation can only go so far. You can't always develop an immediate profile on anyone, especially if you're working with them for the first time. I often tell my clients that, beyond doing your homework, global leaders should be patient and "listen with ten eyes." The Chinese character for *listen*, pronounced "ting" 聽, is made up of three symbols: one ear, ten eyes, and one heart. To understand the truth, one must observe with the ears, eyes, and mind. Sometimes what is not said can be more important than what is said. Sometimes silence is worth its weight in gold.

I'd like to share a few experiences I've come across as an executive coach in dealing with culture and the need to have cultural agility.

"God Willing! No Problem!"

Prabal, an Indian-American executive, jets to the Middle East to lead a management team at a large bank. The first few weeks in Oman go well. Prabal enjoys the beautiful culture and his warm, welcoming colleagues. Then he drills down to the real work at hand: major financial projects that cannot wait. To his surprise, his bank colleagues do not share the American or Asian work ethos. His team shows no urgency about tackling their tasks, and their projects often go unfinished. His Middle Eastern colleagues jokingly say they follow what they call the "IBM Principles," or Inshallah! ("God willing!"), Bukra! ("Tomorrow!"), and Mafi mush-killa! ("No problem!")

Following the AAA model, Prabal reflects on his own cultural values as an American manager (Aware) and learns more about Middle Eastern cultural values to better understand his colleagues (Acquire). Then he introduces his bank team to new, productive work habits (Adapt). "I paired them with other global team members to experience how high-performing teams work together to complete projects," Prabal said. "The most popular part of the training? Flying to the United States, India, and Singapore to learn with global teams." As a result, the team's performance has improved significantly.

Let's throw another wrinkle into the occasion. How about working with different cultures and dealing with millennials—talk about a challenge!

THINK YOU KNOW MILLENNIALS? THINK AGAIN.

For foreign managers, Chinese millennials present a unique set of management challenges. China has gone through tremendous economic and cultural change in the last fifty years.

One of the biggest value shifts has occurred between older and younger generations. Chinese millennials, age eighteen to thirty-five, represent 385 million people, or 28 percent of the population. By 2025, 75 percent of the workforce in China will be millennials.

I have coached and worked closely with Chinese leaders and employees across multiple generations. In this role, I have noticed several trends that distinguish the younger Chinese population from their older colleagues. Younger, urban Chinese tend to be more influenced by global trends than older, more rural Chinese. They tend to be more individualistic, direct, and open. They are entrepreneurial, mobile-dependent, and tech-savvy. And they are most likely the only child in their families.

If you're a foreign manager working with Chinese "knowledge workers" across generations, how do you earn their respect? What do they expect from their managers? The following tips can help foreign managers bridge the generational—and international—divide with millennial Chinese workers.

Show caring and warmth. Good managers in China are often seen as parental figures to their employees. They maintain a delicate balance of establishing authority as the boss and showing personal concern for their employees. For example, showing consideration for the family situations of your employees can demonstrate that you are a well-rounded leader who has the qualities required for managing effectively in this relationship-oriented society.

Know your business. Chinese employees expect their managers to have strong technical knowledge and business acumen. They tend to expect clear directions from their boss. Share information about business direction, vision, and strategies with your employees on a regular basis.

Seek input. Although Chinese employees expect a manager to "be in charge," they also appreciate it when managers ask for their ideas and opinions before making decisions. Chinese workers respect a manager who takes the time to listen to them and sincerely considers their suggestions. However, after seeking input, leaders must clearly communicate the decision and roadmap to employees. Young Chinese employees want to provide input but, ultimately, rely on their boss for guidance and to make the final decision.

Understand "face." The concept of "face" plays an important role in business and society. Face is about dignity, status, prestige, respect, and honor all at once. To "save face" with Chinese employees, never criticize their ideas in front of a group or put them on the spot in a way that may cause embarrassment. To "honor face" and build relationships, show proper respect and genuinely appreciate their contributions.

The stereotype that the Chinese are shy, self-deprecating, and humble has some truth to it. When receiving a compliment, the Chinese tend to brush it off, saying things like "I am not as good as you think" or "My accomplishment is nothing compared to yours." But these comments don't reveal the whole truth. Inside, they may accept the compliment and agree with you, ultimately thriving on such feedback.

Demonstrate maturity. Talking too much may be perceived as a sign of immaturity or ignorance. Take the time to listen and get to know your employees. Avoid showing strong, negative emotions, such as anger or aggression. The Chinese respect those who control their emotions in public. Managers should lead by example by modeling the professional behaviors they expect their employees to demonstrate.

Show interest in your employees' development. Have conversations with your employees about their future with the company and their career paths. Take the time to coach them on their work performance and provide both positive and constructive feedback to help them improve. The talent market is very competitive, and Chinese workers appreciate their bosses showing interest in their professional and career development. Foreign managers must take the time to get to know their millennial employees, understand what motivates them, treat them with respect, take their input seriously, and build trust.

If you do all this, you will do more than "save face." You will earn your employees' respect and loyalty.

HEAR ONE, UNDERSTAND TEN

There are many ways to express "no" in Japanese culture, but saying the word "no" is not one of them. Doing business on an international scale requires understanding that communication styles differ around the globe. You not only have to read between the lines when communicating but you also have to be able to adjust to each culture's style. Nowhere is this more apparent than in the difference between American and Japanese cultures when it comes to expressing the word "no."

One of my clients, Andrew, recently experienced this firsthand.

Andrew is a marketing manager for a global pharmaceutical company. He works closely with colleagues in Japan and the United States. At a recent coaching session, he expressed that he was frustrated and upset, and recounted this story as the reason why.

Andrew had recently asked his Japanese team member Kenji if he thought a proposal Andrew had been developing would be accepted by their colleagues in Japan. Kenji replied, "It may be difficult."

Andrew thought Kenji's reply meant there would be challenges—something he expected. He thought it meant they would have to work harder. So they did. Andrew and his American colleagues worked on the proposal for several more weeks. Eventually, Andrew learned that Kenji never thought the proposal had a chance.

"Why didn't he just come out and tell me, 'No, I don't think it will succeed'?" Andrew said. "We were just wasting our time!"

What happened here? Did Kenji try to trick him? Or did Andrew misinterpret his message? The answer lies in two very nuanced, culturally different approaches to the word "no."

Americans often avoid "no" because they believe saying it will hurt someone's feelings. But in the end, they also believe it can be much more harmful to not tell someone the honest truth, and a straightforward "no" is the best option.

Japanese culture is quite different. They avoid a direct "no." I asked my good friend Diana K. Rowland, Japan expert and author of the book *Japanese Business: Rules of Engagement*, to explain the Japanese resistance to "no."

She said Japanese society is close-knit. Social harmony is always the first priority. "No" can sound like a rejection of the other person, which damages that harmony. Confrontation is considered rude, and keeping good relations with everyone is important.

A similar mentality also applies to the cultures of other Asian countries, such as China and the Philippines. Instead of saying "no," the people of these cultures may make a statement that means no, but sounds ambiguous. "It's not impossible" might mean "I would rather avoid it." "Let me think about it" could mean "The answer is no." This lack of directness applies to more than just "no." Someone might say, "Do you have any plans to come to this area?" and mean "Can you come to my office?"

Agreement might also be delivered differently. You might hear "I get your point," "I am listening," "What is the next step?" and "Hai, hai" instead of "I agree completely." The bottom line? Effective communication with people of Asian cultures requires listening "between the lines."

A classic Japanese saying is "Hear one, understand ten." For each point expressed, the listener is expected to understand at least nine others by implication. Since the most important part of conversation is often unspoken, it becomes the responsibility of the listener to pick up on what has been implied.

When doing business in Asia, it's important to use your inner "antenna" to stay on the same wavelength with others and read or detect their unspoken thoughts and intentions. You must be able to interpret subtle gestures and facial expressions.

In Japan, very little is random, so hold back, listen, watch, and get a trusted colleague to fill you in on the things you may be missing. Eventually, if you are patient enough and humble enough, you'll start to see clues. Then, you will be able to "hear one, understand ten."

Working cross-culturally can certainly be a challenge, particularly when the concept of saving face is especially strong in Asian cultures, but with the AAA method and listening with ten eyes, a global leader can navigate these waters and tap into the strength of a truly diverse team.

CHAPTER 9

Seeing beyond
the Glass Ceiling

T'S AN EXCITING TIME IN THE WORLD. Women as CEOs, women as prime ministers, women at the head of global organizations—such as Christine Lagarde, who led the International Monetary Fund for eight years and is now leading the European Central Bank—never has there been a time in our history when women have blossomed into positions of such importance and influence.

There is still a ways to go. There's still a wage gap where a woman, on average, makes about 78 percent of what a man does. The world economy is still male dominated, and society continues to uncover the ugliness of sexual harassment and intimidation.

Despite these continuing challenges, women are undeniably making great strides forward as leaders and bursting through the glass ceiling in various fields. Yet with all of this progress, I'd be remiss if we didn't spend some time looking at how a woman's role in the workplace is changing and how face plays a unique role in this new environment.

Fifteen years ago, I was tasked with coaching Dr. Darlene Solomon, who is now the chief technology officer of Agilent.

A graduate of Stanford and M.I.T., she is currently one of the highest-ranking female executives in the technology sector. As Darlene made her way up the chain, she paid her dues and put in time as a research and development lab director for Agilent. When a position opened up for a V.P. post at the company, Darlene took the leap. Despite much competition, she was offered the high-profile position, edging out several (male) candidates and R&D directors.

One of Darlene's first major tasks? She needed to establish a positive working relationship with a number of male colleagues who had applied for the same position that she eventually won. While many leaders in her position typically clean house and install their own handpicked team, Darlene valued the experience and knowledge of the existing Agilent R&D team and wanted to keep them together.

I met with Darlene at a popular Palo Alto lunch spot and, in the process of enjoying our calamari steaks, coached her to build closer ties with her male colleagues and humbly ask for their support during her transition. She met individually with each male executive. She listened to their concerns. She told them that she respected their knowledge and experience and that she enjoyed working with them. After all the meetings, Darlene wondered whether they would stay, as partners and peers, to help her develop the new team. To her great delight, each R&D director pledged his support, and not one left Agilent. She showed her colleagues that she was authentic and flexible as a leader. I coached Solomon for a year and a half, and what I observed was that she and her colleagues became a cohesive, high-performing team. Rather than alienate her colleagues, Darlene honored and built face for them. A potentially troubling transition turned into a smooth, successful one. And Darlene did all of this as a working mother of two teens, to boot!

Consider the potential issues at hand with this example— Darlene was tasked to work with colleagues who had applied for the same position she ended up getting in an industry dominated by men. How would they respond to her leadership? Could her gender create any conflicts?

Darlene's approach of treating her team with humility and genuine respect saved face and set the table for a strong team dynamic. While managing a number of male colleagues who had sought the position she ended up getting was an awkward situation, saving and protecting their face was a perfect approach to developing a strong team.

Let's take another example and see how things can easily fall apart. This case of a female American scientist and four male engineers from China has the added complexity of working cross-culturally.

The team leader was Danika, a female scientist in her early thirties, with several advanced degrees, who had been working for a multinational company for eight years as a project leader in Texas. By all accounts she was very friendly and expressive, and came across as confident and smart. Because of her youthful appearance and high energy, she also at times seemed girlish or feminine. She had a great track record with the company and, in her eight years with them, had been promoted three times.

Her peers were four Chinese engineers, all male, who worked in a design office in Shanghai. The four men were in their thirties and forties, had been working together for many years, and spent time together socially as well.

Danika was named as the project leader of a group that included the four Chinese colleagues in Shanghai. They were charged with coming up with design solutions for one of the company's key products. Danika had met her Chinese colleagues in the past, but her interaction with these four had been fairly superficial and didn't include much information about their respective duties. In the course of the group's work, Danika often met with their client. Her four colleagues didn't have any contact with the client.

Another senior engineer who served as Danika's mentor was currently working in the same location as the four engineers.

As a first point of order, Danika set up a meeting with her peers and traveled to Shanghai to meet directly with the team. She set out an agenda that included overall goals for the team, with suggested milestones and specific deadlines for the team to meet. Her Chinese colleagues smiled and quietly jotted down some notes, asking very few questions.

A few weeks after that first meeting, Danika assembled the group for a virtual meeting to discuss their progress. Unfortunately, things didn't seem to be in sync between her and the team. While some of the milestones weren't complete, other activities had been worked on that weren't in the scope of her original plans.

After reviewing the work that had been done against what was supposed to have been done, Danika scheduled a follow-up virtual meeting to discuss why both sides weren't on the same page. Danika encouraged her colleagues to share their thoughts, and, after some coaxing, one of the engineers, Zhang Wei, spoke up.

Very politely, Zhang Wei said, "Thank you for meeting with us. We look forward to working with you, but we don't understand the methodology you're using in approaching this project. Your methodology may be fine, but we have never done it that way."

Danika began sharing how she approached her work. She spoke about how she had been very successful in the past, and that her customers had repeatedly expressed their appreciation for her efforts. The engineers also shared their approach and how it had served them well in the past. Very politely, they said that they felt they would be best served by following their usual procedure and routines. "Danika, if you want to use your methodology, that is okay. We can use our methodology, and you use yours, and we will work in parallel to see which one works better," Zhang said.

After listening to their ideas, and with an eye toward keeping the peace, Danika felt that her approach should be the way to go, but that in order for them all to work together, they should try to accommodate each other and do what needed to be done to reach common goals. The Chinese group nodded, didn't say much, but seemed to agree. In the end, Danika felt that as long as they got the work done, it didn't really matter which approach they used.

After a few weeks, Danika noticed that she was not in the communication loop for a couple of key issues and had not been invited to participate in a recent team meeting. She would share her progress but they didn't share theirs. When she asked about their progress reports, Zhang and his colleagues responded, "We are still working on it. It is not ready . . ." When she asked them for feedback on how she, the project leader, could better support them, their reply was, "Thank you for asking, Danika. You are very nice and cheerful."

She was increasingly concerned and frustrated, so she requested another team conference call. They all replied at the last second and said that something had come up and that they couldn't attend the meeting.

Three and a half months passed, and Danika continued to run the project but still didn't get any progress reports, even after two additional requests to her team to get updates from them. She offered to work with them and coordinate the meetings. But she was getting stonewalled. There was never any confrontation or disagreement. She was just cut out of the loop.

After another month, her manager gave her feedback that she needed to improve her communication skills and needed to be open to new ideas; if she didn't understand something, she needed to ask for clarification.

And then her boss told her that she would be removed from the team.

What, if anything, could Danika have done in the beginning to put this collaboration on the right track? After she sensed that things were not working well, what could she have done to set things right? Was there a need for compromise here, or not? Was there a need to save face here? If so, for whom? What does the BUILD model tell you about this?

There are solutions to this challenge—notice that "solutions" is plural. There is more than one problem in this situation, but fortunately, there is more than one solution.

What should Danika have done before it got to this point?

In the very beginning, Danika should probably have asked more questions to better understand the scope of the project. She could have proactively described her methodology in greater detail, provided historical data on how her customers responded to her approach, and what they liked. Then Danika could have worked collaboratively with Zhang Wei and her other colleagues to decide on a unified approach, instead of going forward in two separate ways.

Danika could also not have made any assumptions about how things were going. She could have realized that her colleagues were being polite and didn't want her to lose face by disagreeing with her, but they also weren't convinced that her approach was the best way forward. She could have made sure both sides understood their respective approaches and confirmed what each side would do and how they would do it. Once they as a team had come to a conclusion, they could have gone to their boss to tell him of their plans. That way, everyone would know that there was no wiggle room and that a plan had been agreed upon.

From an interpersonal standpoint, when Danika went to Shanghai to meet with the engineers, she could have invited them to dinner and spent more time socializing and getting to know them personally. In her interactions with them, she could have talked less about what she wanted, and instead could have asked more questions and listened to their concerns and ideas. These behaviors demonstrate respect (honoring face) and help to build trust and relationships.

Danika could have been more sensitive to the engineers' nonverbal body language, especially when they were silent or indirect. Don't assume silence means agreement. If someone says, "I will try," that often means hesitation.

She could have found ways to build relationships and to talk regularly with her team. She could proactively have offered tips about the client, helped the engineers become more visible to the client, and even introduced them to the client. More familiarity with the client would have given them a better understanding of what they needed to accomplish.

Once they started working on the project with an agreed-upon approach, they needed to have regular meetings for updates and communicate status from both sides. Danika needed to be careful about how she was being perceived. She needed to build the credibility of her technical expertise as well as her leadership.

If she sensed that there was any disengagement, she needed to seek out mentors who understand that culture to help bridge the gap. Miscommunication and assumptions hurt the project. While Zhang Wei and his colleagues felt that she was defying them, in reality she had missed their cues. She needed to clarify their position. She could have asked the other Chinese engineer who had served as her mentor to help mediate between her and the group.

In this example, much of the conflict and misunderstandings happened because both sides retreated to what they were comfortable with and made assumptions based on their own experiences and predilections. Danika would have done better to make the effort to understand the motivations of Zhang Wei and his colleagues, and to interact with them in a more proactive way.

You may notice that these stories don't have an explicit gender bias at play. In fact, in terms of saving or protecting face, these stories could appear in any other place throughout this book. That is true, but it's also important to consider that, setting aside blatant examples of gender discrimination, gender bias is typically far more subtle.

In these examples, protecting and saving face are ways for women in leadership to proactively deal with potential issues, regardless of the underlying influence.

Here's a story of a female executive who successfully navigated around a potentially embarrassing expression of cultural slang.

FACE, PRIDE, AND EGO: HOW FACE TAKES ON MANY MEANINGS

In Asian culture, there is a belief that it is difficult to restore a loss of face. But before one can lose face, what is really lost is the perception of one's own abilities, which some people call pride while others may call it ego.

I don't happen to believe that pride and especially ego are negative things. In fact, I think that belief in oneself is an essential part of taking on challenges and accomplishing important things. What good is it to take on a task if you don't believe you're up to it? Only when a false sense of pride or an inflated ego gets in the way of getting things done does it become negative.

Going deeper than just pride or ego, the idea of face also involves the perspective of those who feel that the actions of others have diminished their own sense of integrity and ability. It just can't be overstated how important the value of face is when working with people of diverse backgrounds.

A perfect example of how to save face comes from my client and good friend Patty McKay, a successful global executive based in the United States. A few years ago, she was a senior leader with a major South Korean–based corporation. Here is her story.

> Once a year at headquarters, they have an annual training about ethics and values. It is taken very seriously. My boss gave me a PowerPoint file from headquarters and said to me, "Your job is to turn this into a training program for all the employees in the States."
>
> I went through all the slides, which included a leadership model. This year, the leadership model was to tell people "We need our leaders to Communicate, Organize their people, Motivate their people, and Empower their people." An acronym was created—the "COME" model. I thought it was a joke! How could I teach this COME model to all the U.S. managers, telling them, "We need all the leaders to COME together to build a stronger culture. Let's all COME every day at work . . ." I thought they must not be serious. "I will not teach our leaders how to COME!!" But no one at the Korean headquarters understood the connotation.
>
> After some thought, I decided to reorganize the model to be an "E-COM" model. When the altered name was presented to the American division, they were in total agreement (after much laughter).

The following week, I made the presentation to a group of Korean managers who happened to be all men and told them we had decided to change the leadership model to E-COM. They said, "No, we can't change it. It is the headquarters' decision. We have to keep it the way it is. Why do you want to change it? What's wrong with the COME model?"

I was too embarrassed to tell them verbally and in front of everyone. I said, "Well, there is another meaning of the word *come* in English. It is impolite to discuss it in the group." So I wrote down on a piece of paper, "Another meaning for the word 'come' is 'orgasm.'" I handed them the piece of paper and left the room.

I stood outside the room and heard a lot of discussion. Then someone came out to tell me, "Okay. We will teach the E-COM model in the United States."

I've learned by working with Koreans that you should never embarrass Korean men. Writing down the meaning on a piece of paper helped all of us to save face. I also needed to manage the gender sensitivity. As a female manager, I spared myself from having to explain to them about a slang word with a sexual meaning.

AN AMAZING LESSON
FROM AN AMAZING WOMAN

Women are experiencing a time of momentous change. In boardrooms and offices around the country, they are realizing their true power and potential. As a leadership coach, I have worked with and been inspired by thousands of successful women leaders from around the world. Although these women come from different walks of life, they share many habits, behaviors, points of view, and attitudes that have led them to where they are today.

In her 2018 Golden Globe speech, Oprah Winfrey referred to today as a "new dawn" for women. To guide you through this new dawn, here are two key pieces of advice for women leaders, based on what I have learned from the incredible women I've met and worked with throughout my career.

Step up and speak up

In the workplace, some women shy away from attention. They stay in their box. They wait for an invitation to excel beyond their assigned roles, for permission to make themselves known.

As women leaders, we must learn how to raise our hands. We must make ourselves more visible. Don't wait for someone to pick you, invite you, or give you permission to get involved. Tell people you want to be involved. Share your accomplishments, your achievements, even your dreams and goals.

One of the most remarkable women I have ever met is Frances Hesselbein, the former CEO of the Girl Scouts of the USA. At 103 years old, Frances is still actively speaking and writing, and serves today as the president and CEO of the Frances Hesselbein Leadership Institute. I met Frances thirty years ago. Reflecting on her remarkable career, I asked her if she had had a plan when she started her journey. "No," she replied. "I didn't have a career plan. But what I did was whenever there was a door open and a new opportunity, I always looked into it and took a chance and walked through the door."

Those opportunities arise only if people know you are looking for them, if you make your intentions and your goals known to the world. Step up and speak up, and opportunity will find you. You then have to be bold enough to take it.

Modulate your "dimmer switch"

Some women do the opposite of shying away. Their light switch is either on or off, all or nothing. You often hear these people say things like, "This is who I am. Take it or leave it."

As a leader, you must learn to read your audience and tailor your message to the listener. If you are perceived as overbearing to a particular audience, your message will not be received well. Think of your attitude and behaviors as being on a dimmer switch that you can brighten or dim, depending on the audience. Be flexible and work in a range that is appropriate to the situation. Learn how to modulate your brightness.

When I met Frances Hesselbein, I noticed that she always paused for two seconds before responding to a comment or question. After observing this behavior several times, I realized what she was doing. She was taking a moment to think through her response, to adjust her message for her audience. She was taking a moment to modulate her dimmer switch.

FOUR WAYS TO EMPOWER YOURSELF
AS A WOMAN IN BUSINESS

In a world of gender imbalance in the boardroom, women can still show up with confidence, control, and authority. Here are a few fundamental steps women can take to navigate in today's business world.

I was recently invited to deliver a keynote speech for the annual conference of the Women Presidents' Organization (WPO), an organization for women presidents, CEOs, and managing directors of privately held, multimillion-dollar companies. Before the conference, I asked attendees to submit questions they'd like answered. Several people asked a variation of this question:

"In some countries I work in, it's extremely rare to see women in senior executive positions sitting at boardroom tables. How can I be successful in countries where female CEOs or business owners are not expected or respected?"

Unfortunately, this is a reality women continue to deal

with around the world, and being hardworking, smart, and having business savvy isn't enough. But when they conduct business anywhere, there are steps women can take to feel empowered and to establish and hold on to their credibility.

1. **Create a command presence.** A first impression is often built on appearance. Sadly, this is especially true for women in business. For this reason, I recommend women create a neutral appearance, one that does not distract or detract from their authority. Opt for minimal accessories, clothing that is not too revealing, and a professional dress code—an appearance that says "listen to me," and not "look at me." Similarly, a strong physical "command presence" communicates you are in control. First, stand up straight, with feet slightly apart, chest open, shoulders back, and chin up. Then, shake it up and do it again. This is the ideal—a more relaxed, natural "command presence" that presents confidence and ease.

2. **Understand and use hierarchy.** People of every culture pick up subtle cues that convey hierarchy. Use this to your advantage and enlist the help of your male colleagues to consistently communicate the status of your position. Have them introduce you with your proper professional title, and make sure that title is stated clearly on your business card. In hierarchical cultures, if a question is asked, the most senior person answers it. Speak to your colleagues ahead of time so that they defer questions to you—this helps to continuously cement your position as the person in charge.

3. **Don't accidentally give in to gender stereotypes.** There are some gender stereotypes we are aware of, and there are some that are so mundane they're almost subconscious behaviors. But these behaviors can undermine your authority the most. For example, resist the urge to bring coffee to your

colleagues, or casually clear dishes after a lunch meeting. You may think you are just being courteous, but to many people from different cultures, those behaviors say, "I'm not actually the leader, I'm an assistant."

4. **Show up like an accomplished veteran.** When you've made it to the leadership level, you're established and accomplished in your career and you should present yourself that way. You have the benefit of experience. You look back and forward. You are confident, comfortable in your own skin, and a dynamic storyteller with an extensive library of examples. You are not ashamed to tell stories of your failures—in fact, you relish in sharing how you learned from them. Channel these qualities and you only reinforce your status further.

The business world, in the United States and internationally, still has a long way to go to achieve complete gender equality. But, as a female entrepreneur or leader, you have the tools today to empower yourself, and inspire the generations that will follow you.

FIVE WAYS TO SUCCEED
OUTSIDE YOUR COMFORT ZONE

If you're anything like me, you sometimes feel like a fish out of water. Maybe you moved to a new country, took a new job, or found yourself in some situation that forced you outside your comfort zone and into new—and awkward—territory. Over the course of my career as an executive coach specializing in cross-cultural management and global leadership, I've come to see this as a good thing. New situations teach you to adapt—which ultimately gives you a competitive edge. Leaders who embrace change and uncertainty learn to:

1. Focus on what they can control (and not on what they can't)

2. Stretch themselves to learn new things

3. Give their teams stretch assignments or challenging tasks

4. Discover new business opportunities and creative solutions

5. Be okay with failure, as long as people don't make the same mistake twice

These skills have made a critical difference for some of the world's most successful leaders.

Indra Nooyi, the first female CEO of PepsiCo, was born in India and climbed the corporate ladder in a foreign country and culture. She boosted revenue 80 percent during her tenure at PepsiCo.

Alan Mulally left Boeing to become CEO of Ford Motor Company—leaping into a new industry that was then in mid-collapse. He adapted quickly and accomplished a historic turnaround, without the government bailout that saved other automakers.

Elon Musk launched Tesla in Silicon Valley, not Detroit, and changed the paradigm for car companies.

When I was twenty-two, I moved from Taiwan to the United States to attend graduate school at the University of Pennsylvania, and later worked as a management consultant. I loved the work, but when I looked around at the other people in my field, I saw only white men in their forties, fifties, and sixties. I wondered why no one else looked like me. I began to think the job wasn't the right fit.

I mentioned this discomfort to my mentor, the well-known executive coach Marshall Goldsmith. He thought about it for a while and then said, "You might think it's a disadvantage to be young, Asian, and female in this field, but I think these are actually advantages."

After all, he said, I spoke fluent English and Chinese, and

I had a multicultural background that was ideal for helping leaders work in a global environment. I began to understand that being different can be good. Why try to think and act like a middle-aged white man? I should just be myself. As a result, I've had a fascinating journey through a career I love. Sometimes I still feel like the odd one out—but now I know that's a good thing.

The truth is, everyone has a bout of lacking self-confidence from time to time. For women, when their professional ladder may seem steeper than others, such times can be especially self-defeating. Women already have enough challenges to realizing their potential in today's workplace. The last thing they need is for their own negative internal dialogue to be holding them back. For those women out there who sometimes feel like a fish out of water, I know how you feel. Take comfort in knowing that you are where you belong, and the future is a bright one.

BE YOUR OWN
CHEERING SQUAD

As I work with clients to help them become the leaders they want to be, I often find that the single thing holding them back—or pushing them forward—is what they tell themselves. We act on the things we tell ourselves. Here's how to make that internal dialogue work for you.

Take, for example, my client Carissa, a high-tech professional on the path to a leadership position. Carissa, who holds a Harvard MBA, has a promising career. Her company has flagged her as a high-potential leader and enrolled her in a robust leadership program.

During our first coaching session, I asked Carissa what she'd like to work on. "I constantly self-sabotage," she replied. "I put myself down all the time and I don't see my own worth."

This ongoing internal dialogue affected how she presented herself at work. When Carissa facilitated meetings, she used self-deprecating phrases like "I'm not an expert," "I'm not sure if this is right," and "I may be wrong." This language immediately tells her audience, "I don't believe in myself. You shouldn't believe in me, either."

Carissa's internal dialogue affected her nonverbal communication, too. When she's not leading a meeting, she tends to sit in the back of the room, out of sight, sending the message that she does not belong—even though her education, experience, and performance more than prove that she does.

There are many cultural, sociological, and personal reasons behind the things we say to ourselves. But one thing is universally true: Our internal dialogue can become so powerful that it can change the way we live our lives. The story you tell yourself can hold you back, or it can power you to move forward. Here are some strategies to help you change your story.

Identify your story. Many of us are not aware of our internal dialogue. The first step is figuring out what we're telling ourselves, and making sure it's helping, not hurting. What do you say to yourself after a success? After a failure? How do you approach high-stress situations—do you build yourself up, or tear yourself down?

Develop a growth mindset. According to researcher Carol Dweck, there are two types of mindsets—a fixed mindset and a growth mindset.[1] People who hold fixed mindsets believe their talents and abilities are permanently in place, inflexible to change. In contrast, people with growth mindsets focus on the future. They believe their talents and abilities can grow and develop. Our internal dialogue can reflect a fixed mindset ("I'm just not good at public speaking") or a growth mindset ("With some practice, I'll be a great public speaker").

Think in the "now." People often place conditions on their happiness or readiness for success—"I'll be happy when I get a different job," or "I'll be confident at work once I have enough experience." This type of thinking may focus on the future, but it is limiting. It keeps us from living in the moment, from taking the experience, knowledge, and confidence we have now and using it as fuel for growth.

Treat yourself with respect. When you find yourself engaging in internal dialogue, ask yourself, is this something I would say to a friend? A colleague? A family member? If it's something you wouldn't say to someone you respect, don't say it to yourself. The inspirational George Raveling, Nike's former Director of International Basketball, said it best: "Most relationships come with an expiration date. The most important relationship you will ever have is the relationship you have with yourself."

Be intentional. In his book *Triggers*, executive coach and author Marshall Goldsmith describes how, at the end of each day, he asks himself a set of questions about health, relationships, and professional matters. The questions start with the phrase "Have I done my best"—for example, "Have I done my best today to build positive relationships?" Are there any areas of your life that can benefit from specific, intentional self-messaging? Replacing negative, self-sabotaging internal dialogue with questions like these can lead us on a more proactive, positive path.

Meditate with a mantra. Marshall's questions are intentional. Another way to integrate a daily intention is through meditation, specifically with a mantra that focuses us in a positive direction. Deepak Chopra has authored many of my favorite mantras, including "Everything I desire is within me" and "I move through my days light-hearted and carefree, knowing all is well." As I meditate, I use these mantras as reminders of my intention, reminders that as I change my internal dialogue—my own story—I change my life.

COMBATING
MICRO-INEQUITIES AT WORK

Believing in yourself and not holding yourself back is only about you. But at times, those you work with can do things, whether they know it or not, that can keep you from reaching your potential. Small, subtle behaviors that overlook, single out, or discount someone, often based on unconscious biases against characteristics like race and gender, are called "micro-inequities," a term coined in 1973 by MIT professor Mary Rowe.[2] Here is an example of these, along with things you can do to make your voice heard.

One of my clients is experiencing a professional obstacle that is, unfortunately, all too common. Susan is a passionate, driven, high-performing leader in a technology company. Although she often has a seat at the table with other company leaders, she finds that she doesn't have a voice there. Susan is often interrupted and finds her contributions brushed off or—worse—sometimes her ideas are at first ignored, only to be repeated by a colleague the next day, or even fifteen minutes later, at which point they are enthusiastically embraced by the team.

Behaviors like these can be described as micro-inequities. It's not up to Susan to rewrite her colleagues' unconscious biases. And it's the job of everyone in the company to create a more inclusive environment. But there are things Susan can do to take back her power in the situation. These are steps you can take, too, if you ever find yourself in a similar predicament.

Change your mindset about "bragging"

Susan has accomplished extraordinary things with her team. She rightfully has a place at the table with company leadership. But that doesn't necessarily mean other leaders know what she's done. Without that established credibility, her colleagues may not be eager to hear her ideas. I asked Susan why she hasn't shared her successes with company leaders.

"I am British," she responded. "I don't want to brag."

Being uncomfortable "bragging"—or self-promoting—can be tied to culture as well as gender. Studies often find that women find it more difficult to tout their achievements than men do, even at the senior level.

If self-promotion feels uncomfortable, change your mindset about it. You are doing more than promoting yourself—you are promoting your team. Instead of "bragging," frame it this way: "I'm sharing the team's accomplishments so we can build on this momentum to push things forward, so it benefits the entire company." If you take the focus off of yourself and put it on the organization, you may feel more confident promoting your achievements. How are you and your team helping customers, increasing market share, and benefiting the organization overall?

Get buy-in from key stakeholders

Susan often feels like a lone wolf in the boardroom, the only person who is aware of the value she brings. I recommended that she work on building alliances with colleagues, so they can support her when she speaks up and vouch for her value as a peer.

To understand the power of this kind of buy-in, consider this anecdote about the women in the Obama White House. When President Obama took office, two-thirds of his top aides were men. His female aides complained of being ignored and talked over during meetings. So they adopted a strategy: When a woman offered an idea or insight, other women would repeat what she said, while also making sure to attach her name to the idea. This strategy, which they called "amplification," forced the men in the room to recognize the contributions of their female colleagues.

If Susan gets buy-in from key stakeholders in her company, she can have her own "amplification" system.

Look at your own subconscious behaviors

Micro-inequities are behaviors delivered and perceived at a subconscious level. Susan, too, was communicating subconscious messages that were holding her back.

First, we analyzed her patterns of speech. At the senior level, many executives prefer communication that is succinct. Susan's technical background cultivated a way of communicating that was much more thorough, detailed, and lengthy. We worked on refining her messages so that they better matched the communication style of her peers, which made it easier for them to receive and appreciate her messages.

Second, we considered her nonverbal communication. Was she sitting up straight, with open body language, projecting ease and confidence? Where she sat in the room also communicated a message. When people sit in an outer ring or off in a corner, away from the seats at a conference table, they communicate that they're outsiders—and they're difficult to hear and see. I encouraged Susan to position herself in the center, sending the subconscious message that not only does she belong but also she deserves to have the attention of the entire room.

Just to bring it back full circle, what impact do these micro-inequities have on those who experience them? They cause a loss of face, whether they are meant to or not. Saving face is not only about what you can do to avoid having others lose face. It's also about taking actions that keep you from losing yours.

CHAPTER 10

Face and the
Value of Feedback

T'S TIME to get to the crux of the matter by asking a pain-
fully obvious question: What is it that leaders do?

For those of you who are thinking, "Duh! They lead!
That's why they're a LEADER!" Well, what can I say?
You're absolutely right.

How do the best leaders find success doing what they do?
Anyone who has successfully managed a group of people,
whether it's a small office or a Global Fortune 500 company,
knows that a true leader does more than simply tell others
what to do. At the very least, if you've read this far into this
book, you understand how a leader's responsibility is to look
out for not only the company's bottom line but also the bottom line of your staff. The best leader knows you really can't
have one without the other.

In what way is saving face most immediate in the role of
a leader? The answer is . . . in providing feedback. That's the
single most impactful role a leader has with their staff. Do
it correctly, and you can inspire them to reach their highest
potential. Do it without the proper approach, and things can
unravel quickly.

I provide feedback to people for a living. As an executive coach, I work with senior executives from Global 500 companies. One of the first steps I take with anyone is to provide 360-degree feedback to them as part of the coaching process.

For those of you who are unfamiliar with it, 360-degree feedback entails surveying or interviewing the supervisor, peers, and direct reports of the leader who is getting the feedback. As the coach, my job is then to encapsulate the results so that none of the information is attributable to any given person, and then present it to the coachee to give them a sense of how others view their performance. You can probably imagine how tentative and downright stressful it is to receive a report like this. The coachee is opening themself up in a very vulnerable way, and their feelings can sometimes be very emotional and raw.

But the most successful leaders have learned that feedback, both positive and negative, if provided in the right way, can honor face for someone and inspire them to raise their own performance and professional development. Let's look at some of the ways to do just that.

The Untapped Potential of Feedback

Your feedback can build the confidence of your team members—or it can tear them down. Giving feedback is routine for leaders. But don't let the everyday nature of feedback fool you—a single moment of giving feedback can have momentous impact, especially if the way it is delivered results in someone losing face.

Consider one of my clients, Mark. Mark manages Joseph, who is one of his top salespeople. Joseph is from the Philippines and Mark was born and raised in the United States.

On one particular sales call, Joseph was trying to close a large deal with a potential customer. He got ahead of himself in his zeal and made a commitment to provide additional services that weren't normally included in such deals. He also didn't check with his service department before making the commitment.

When Mark learned of this, he told Joseph that the company wasn't prepared or able to provide the additional services Joseph had promised. "In the future, you should check with the service department before offering items outside the normal scope of services," Mark said.

Upon hearing this feedback, Joseph felt as though his actions had jeopardized his future with the company. He submitted his resignation.

Surprised by this reaction, Mark immediately reassured Joseph that he was doing a great job. The feedback had been meant to correct a simple miscalculation and was not a personal attack on Joseph's character. He assured Joseph that he appreciated his work and asked him to stay with the company. Joseph accepted.

Many people often personalize negative feedback, perceiving it to be an attack on their character. They view feedback as a loss of face. While this reaction is pronounced in Asian cultures, it is a natural human response.

In commenting on neuroscience research for her forthcoming book on competencies for working across cultures, author and intercultural expert Diana K. Rowland notes that when we feel threatened, whether physically or emotionally, a distress signal in our brains creates an impulse to fight or flee. We become less able to use our prefrontal cortex, which deals with logic, empathy, and regulating social behavior, and instead react aggressively or defensively. We also create a negative memory, which is stronger and lasts longer than a positive one.

Negative feedback can create this kind of reaction, causing someone to lose face, often irreparably. We can avoid this by following a few guidelines for giving feedback.

Use "straight talk." When delivering feedback, make sure your message is communicated accurately and clearly, and in a way that makes the other person feel respected. Deliver it in a private, safe environment. Make sure the message is based on facts and expectations are clear.

The Center for Creative Leadership developed an effective approach called SBII: Situation→Behavior→Impact→Intent. First, describe the situation. Then, describe the observable behavior and its impact on you—what you thought and/or felt. Finally, inquire about the intention behind the behavior.

For example: "At the staff meeting yesterday, you raised your voice when Sally questioned your financial data. It made me and the team feel uncomfortable about speaking up. What was going through your mind?"

This approach focuses on facts and behaviors. Defensive reactions are minimized, leading to productive conversation, desired outcomes, and no one losing face.

Avoid "blunt talk" and "safe talk." Instead of straight talk, most people use either blunt talk or safe talk to deliver feedback. Neither technique works.

With blunt talk, the person giving feedback doesn't consider whether it's the right time and place to deliver feedback. Clarity and accuracy aren't important. The receiver's feelings aren't considered—the giver just needs to get things off their chest.

The impact of blunt talk is that the receiver does not feel respected and likely feels blamed or unappreciated. Walls are put up, and the feedback is usually difficult to accept.

The receiver becomes so resentful that they don't make the needed changes.

Safe talk is the opposite of blunt talk, but equally damaging. Instead of direct feedback, hints are dropped. The message is vague and ambiguous. The manager thinks that feedback was provided, but the receiver is confused about what was said and may even think everything is fine. The manager may have intended to save face and preserve harmony, but has actually created confusion. The result is the same as with blunt talk—nothing changes.

To ensure feedback is understood and digested, and to preserve the dignity of the receiver, stick to straight talk.

Use positive feedback to "honor face." Honoring face is the opposite of losing face—you build a person's confidence and help them grow. This can be accomplished by giving positive feedback.

In "The Feedback Fallacy," Marcus Buckingham and Ashley Goodall note that managers often give feedback only after something goes wrong.[1] The instinct is to tell someone what they did wrong and how to fix it. This is remediation, which inhibits learning and does not lead to strong performance.

In computer computations, a high-priority interrupt happens when something requires a computer processor's immediate attention, and the machine halts normal operations and jumps the urgent issue to the head of the processing queue. Like computer processors, team leaders have quite a few things that demand their attention and force them to act. Many of them are problems. If you see something go off the rails—a poorly handled call, a missed meeting, a project gone awry—the instinct will kick in to stop everything to tell someone what she did wrong and what she needs to do to fix it. This instinct is by no means misguided: If your team member screws something up, you have to deal with it. But remember that when you do, you're merely remediating—and that remediating not only inhibits learning but also gets you no closer to excellent performance.

Likewise, conjuring excellence from your team members requires a different focus from you. If you see somebody doing something that really works, stopping them and identifying it with her isn't just a high-priority interrupt, it is your highest-priority interrupt. Buckingham and Goodall encourage managers to stop someone when they're doing something well and dissect their behavior or actions with them. This puts them into what they call a "rest and digest" state of mind, which helps them understand what strong performance looks and feels like, and builds confidence—and trust in their manager—in the long term.

Focus on "feedforward," not feedback. Feedforward is the opposite of feedback. Feedback focuses on the past. Feedforward focuses on the future. We can't change the past, but we can create the future. Feedback can be demotivating, while feedforward is empowering. It is necessary to deliver feedback, but don't stop there. To set people up for success, take the time to coach your employees on lessons learned and practical next steps to move things forward.

Feedback is a necessary part of leadership. Use straight talk, give positive as well as negative feedback, include feedforward, and always keep the receiver's dignity and "face" in mind. Then feedback can become one of your most powerful tools.

I like to think about feedback in terms of intent versus impact. Almost every manager goes into their responsibilities with good intentions, but your actions or message can still result in a negative impact. Impact is the only thing that really matters—not intent. When it comes to feedback, think twice about the impact of your words.

LOVE THEM
OR LOSE THEM

Of course, as an executive coach, I'm in the perhaps unusual position of having coachees who want to be coached in the first place. The majority of my clients have made it a priority to put in the time and effort to develop their leadership skills and have asked to work with an executive coach. They want to improve.

As a leader of a team or organization, you won't always know how your team will react to your guidance as a manager. You won't always know how they'll respond to your feedback. And yet, as a leader, it's your responsibility to develop a team that can work to its highest potential. The ability to save face is the first and most important step in a leader's ability to retain talent and have the group work as a team.

If your best people feel supported and appreciated, they're likely to stay.

Research consistently shows that the top reason people leave their jobs isn't related to compensation, benefits, or even opportunities for career growth: It is that they don't feel appreciated.

When saving face is employed authentically, it can strengthen relationships and serve as a social currency. But honoring face can also help create a culture of respect and appreciation, one that can help you retain your best people— and get the best out of them.

Two of my clients have recently had experiences that illustrate how crucial face can be to showing appreciation, building trust, and retaining your best talent.

A shift in perspective

Martha and Beth are colleagues and equal partners working on a strategy project for their company. Martha perceives Beth as not delivering on her end of the work. She feels Beth expects her to do all the work. Martha says Beth holds meetings with others "just to build connections," but shows no tangible results from the meetings. In all, Martha suspects Beth doesn't know how to do the strategy work, but doesn't want to admit it. She says she is saving face for Beth and protecting her credibility.

From Beth's perspective, Martha is pushy, dominant, and not sensitive to others' well-being. In meetings, Martha asks questions, but her tone is condescending: "What are your priorities? What resources do you have? Can you get it done?" Beth feels as though she's drowning, but Martha is not offering help or guidance—she's only taking over the work for Beth.

For Beth to feel respected and appreciated, Martha needs to shift her perspective, realizing that a more collaborative approach will lead to a more productive, positive working relationship. Martha's goal shouldn't be to win or "be right"— she should realize that she and Beth are working toward the same end goal.

I encouraged Martha to be a thought partner to Beth, to frame the project's success as *their* success. Her approach to communication shifted. Instead of asking questions like "When will you get this done?," she emphasized collaboration, support, and a win/win for all: "What would be your top three priorities for Q2 that will bring a big win for you and your team?" "How can I support you?"

I also encouraged Martha to relate to Beth on a more human level—to show genuine interest in her life outside of work. This shift in communication style resulted in Beth feeling safer, less "underwater," and appreciated. In these ways, Martha started to truly save face for Beth.

Moving On from a Mistake

Here's an example of a situation where the loss of face ended up costing a company the skills of a valued staff member.

Carl is a highly successful leadership consultant. Several years ago, he worked for a consulting firm that served the private equity industry. The firm was preparing feedback on an organizational audit that included evaluations on the effectiveness of each member of the client's executive team. Carl was tasked with compiling the aggregate results.

Unfortunately, when Carl forwarded the information to the client, he provided a spreadsheet rather than a PDF—this allowed more technologically savvy members of the executive team to trace the feedback back to the individuals who provided it, completely exposing them and violating confidentiality agreements.

Carl's error threatened to jeopardize the entire project and the client's trust in them as partners. "I remember the feeling like it was yesterday," he recalls. "I remember walking in the door of my house, saying to myself, 'I'm going to get fired, I'm going to get fired.'"

Fortunately, his company's IT team was able to recall the message and destroy the data before it could get into more hands. Carl accepted full responsibility. While the company CEO was forgiving, the private equity partner was not. He called Carl's manager and demanded he be fired. His manager stood up for him, asserting his value on the team.

Carl continued through to the end of the project, but everything had changed. During later face-to-face sessions, the private equity partner would not make eye contact with him.

Carl soon left the firm, and feels the experience left a scar. "My suspicion has always been that sooner or later, the managing director of our firm would have let me go. He'd protected me externally, but he no longer believed in me as a strong A-player," he says.

The truth is, Carl was an A-player who had simply made a mistake. Everyone makes mistakes—it's how we respond to those mistakes, as managers, that affects a worker's later performance. Carl's firm did not help him feel supported. They could not help him save face, and for that reason they could not retain him. When a mistake happens, how a manager or organization deals with it can make or break relationships.

If we want to retain our best talent and help them do their best work, we must build them up—using techniques such as high-priority interrupts—rather than belittle them. We must help them save face and learn from it when mistakes inevitably happen. Retaining great talent is about more than compensation—it's about respect, support, and face.

EMPATHY

As I mentioned earlier, as a leader, you won't always know how your team will react in a given situation. Part of the benefit of being culturally agile is being able to tune into the needs and concerns of the moment. Here are a few interesting real-life examples of cultural agility at work—or sometimes not!

Not too long ago, I worked on an important global leadership program for a German client and was part of a multicultural faculty team, many of whom were based in Europe. We were in Wiesbaden, Germany, all working together on the project for the first time. We had to work late in the day in order to prepare for the following days' activities.

We started doing all the prep work for the program very early in the morning and worked through to the late afternoon before taking our first break. Even then, our late lunch would be a working lunch, as we still had a lot of development work to do.

It was a sweltering summer day in Wiesbaden, and my first instinct was to find a quiet, air-conditioned corner of the hotel's cafeteria so that we could all work and eat in comfort. But as I sat down with my lunch, I noticed that my German colleagues were all standing by the door next to the outdoor patio, looking a bit crestfallen as they saw a number of us sit down in the air-conditioned room. When I asked them what was going on, they said they were hoping that we could do the working lunch outside, where it was nice and sunny.

Being based in Southern California, where we have, on average, 38 days of rain a year with 266 days of sunshine year round, the last thing I wanted to do was to sit outside in my business attire, eating my schnitzel and working while languishing in the brutal heat of the day! But my German colleagues' perspective was different. Germany's winters can be long and frigid, and this spring's weather had been unseasonably cold. Today's sunshine was the first real warmth the Germans had felt all year long, and they relished the thought of soaking in all the rays. So, in the end, we picked up our trays and moved outside to the covered patio, where the ice-cold sparkling water kept me from melting, and my German colleagues could revel in their sweaty bliss!

While the question of whether to sit outside for a business luncheon is hardly a monumental executive decision, it does show how people's backgrounds and personal histories can inform their perception of everything, even the weather. The ability to show empathy is the ability to understand and recognize those perceptions.

HOW FEEDBACK CAN
LEAD TO STRONGER SOLUTIONS

Bill Bundy is a seasoned business executive and a good friend of mine. He shared a story that indicates how accepting feedback can actually strengthen a project and manage to save face.[2] He shows how negotiation can save face and give stakeholders a gracious way to change their mind so both sides can reach a compromise.

At the time, Bill was working for a large digital curriculum provider and was in the process of proposing an implementation for one of the largest school districts in the country. During his conversations with district leadership, their areas of focus were in decreasing dropout rates, improving graduation rates, and providing optional courses not generally offered by the district.

Bill's company had a solution to fit the bill. Bill's company as well as a number of competitors presented proposals to district stakeholders. After four separate presentations, Bill was confident that their solution stood out in all the areas the school district was focused on.

However, during another evaluation meeting with district leadership, the concern was raised that their solution would invariably replace teachers. This was a serious challenge, because the teachers' union had a very strong presence within the district and the union was certain that teachers' jobs were at risk.

To address this concern, during the next evaluation presentation, Bill brought in a representative from the County Office of Education (COE) who had worked at a large neighboring district implementing a solution similar to what Bill's company was offering; they, too, had to address the union concern. The neighboring district informed the COE that they found they needed additional teachers to support the initial implementation of the project, because the teachers were and are a critical component for the success of the program. They also found that the program successfully augmented the overall school program and increased the need to hire additional teachers. Most important, the data gathered indicated that dropouts had reduced and graduation rates had increased.

Having this additional information, presented and validated by a trusted peer, allowed the decision makers to reconsider their positions and embrace Bill's proposed solution in a way that allowed them to save face. It was a win-win for all involved.

Many companies that may have been wildly successful before venturing out to develop business in other countries naturally stick with how they have done business in the past, because that's what brought them success in the first place. I call it the "That's how we got here!" mentality. But many of my clients soon discover that the complexity of working with partners in other parts of the globe requires rethinking how business needs to be conducted. Let's look at a couple of examples.

HOW NOT TO GET OFF
TO A GOOD START

As the global economy was becoming more competitive in nearly every industry sector, the U.S. furniture industry was in a free fall. American furniture manufacturers, accustomed to producing nearly all of their furniture primarily in North Carolina and surrounding areas, were suddenly faced with

the threat of competing against Chinese furniture manufacturers, who were paying their factory workers a tenth of what
the U.S. manufacturers were paying their own workers. Most
American furniture companies saw the writing on the wall
and realized that the only way they could compete on a global
scale was to transition some or all of their manufacturing
work to China.

When representatives of a major furniture brand first
traveled to visit a Chinese factory in South China, the factory owners greeted the American executives with hot tea and
light snacks, and hosted a dinner at a local restaurant in their
honor. In fact, every time any manager would visit, the factory owners' hospitality would be the same—hot tea, light
snacks, and a meal at a local restaurant.

On the other hand, the American executives' demeanor
was not nearly as welcoming. During meetings, the executives would lay out what their objectives and requirements
were; they spent little time getting to know their new Chinese
partners. What's worse, instead of staying in a hotel near the
factory, they would make a two-hour commute from Hong
Kong. Instead of taking the opportunity to spend more time
getting to know their Chinese counterparts, at the end of
each day the American executives would hightail it back to a
Marriott hotel in Hong Kong and end the day having a steak
dinner every night at Ruth's Chris Steakhouse!

It's understandable that the Chinese factory owners felt
a loss of face, considering that the only time their American
partners had with them was spent laying out their requirements and demands, and any downtime they had was spent
across the border in Hong Kong, eating expensive steaks at
the most Western of American restaurants. While this was
just the first encounter between the two companies, it indicated how the American company expected to work with its

new Chinese partners, and the relationship immediately had a rocky start.

By way of contrast, here's an example of two companies that made an effort to accommodate each other.

HOW ONE NICE SUIT
DESERVES ANOTHER

In 2005, the Chinese multinational computer company Lenovo purchased IBM's personal computer division. From the outset, the two companies seemed very different in terms of philosophy and culture. Lenovo was a relative newcomer to the computer industry—it started up in Beijing in 1984 and incorporated in Hong Kong in 1988. IBM was and is an American institution—founded in 1911, it is the venerable stalwart of the technology industry and, in terms of employees, is one of America's largest businesses.

As one of Lenovo's executives shared with me, on the first day that Lenovo's executives met with IBM's executives, no one knew exactly what to expect. As he told the story: "As both sides greeted each other, our team noticed that all the IBM folks were wearing polo shirts and khaki pants. The IBM group likewise noticed that our group was wearing suits and ties. The rest of the day went very well as both sides looked to develop a strong team for the future. The following day, we got together again, except this time, the IBM executives were all wearing suits and ties and our group came wearing polo shirts and khaki pants! Everyone had a good laugh, and the rest of our meeting went remarkably well."

Lenovo went on to become one of the top PC manufacturers in the world, and recently agreed to acquire a significant share of IBM's server business; in 2014 they decided to purchase Motorola Mobility from Google.

Obviously, the success or failure of any company has

little to do with whether its executives decide to eat steak every night or whether they wear khakis or a suit and tie to work. The point is, each example indicates the willingness of business partners to consider the needs of the other, and whether they are able to show the kind of respect that everyone appreciates.

The old saying "Money doesn't buy you happiness" is a good one. It's certainly true when it comes to you as a leader working to motivate and inspire your team. To retain talent, saving face is the real moneymaker.

CHAPTER 11

Facetime

When we treat people merely as they are,
they will remain as they are. When we treat
them as if they were what they should be,
they will become what they should be.

—THOMAS S. MONSON

E'VE ARRIVED.

No more talk about the BUILD or the AAA model. No more phrases about "psychological safety" or "cultural agility." And no more mentions of the cultural iceberg! This isn't to say that there's not a lot of value in these techniques or descriptions—there is. That's why we've spent the time and effort to share these ideas with you.

But as we near the end of our journey together about saving face, let's take a step back and make sure we can see the forest through the trees. What is the big picture?

When we first came up with the premise for this book, we started with the working title "About Face." I liked the double meaning of the title, where we would be focusing on all the facets of honoring and saving face, and also describing how the act of saving face could "turn around" a bad situation—in military lingo, doing an "about face."

The big picture is all about the possibility of doing an "about face" and what is at the heart of it. Think of a typical offense. I would venture to say that at the heart of every real or perceived offense is the loss of face or a sense that someone has been disrespected.

If you are at a restaurant and the waiter has attended to every other table repeatedly but not yours, I'd wager that your offended feeling has less to do with the extra few minutes you have to wait and more to do with why the waiter seems not to give you the same level of care as others. That's about face.

- If two people are doing the same quality of work, but one of them is getting paid less . . .

- If someone spends weeks researching and writing a proposal and it hardly sees the light of day . . .

- If a manager sends out a communication that inadvertently discloses critical information about another coworker . . .

The first reaction might be, it's not fair, or it's not right, but don't kid yourself—it's all about face. For the person getting paid less even when they're doing an equal amount of work, it doesn't matter if the difference is not financially meaningful. The common refrain is, "It's not about the money. It's the principle." And what is the principle? It's all about face.

But face is just as powerful when it is a positive influence.

Just today, I had a technical issue with my website and I called the company that hosts the website for help. At the end of the call, I had to pay $375 to fix the situation. While I'm never particularly excited about paying for things like this, I also accept that it's just the price of doing business.

About an hour later, I got a call back from the hosting company. It was the same person who had sold me the service earlier. He called to let me know that he was working on the order and realized that he could get the same thing done without having to charge me for one of the services I ordered.

He told me he would be refunding me $300.

Was I happy about saving $300? Of course. But my primary reaction was that this person took the time to look at the situation and figured out a way to accomplish the same thing for less money. It took him additional time and his company would make a little less money. I can only conclude that his only motivation was to be attentive to his customer's needs. He was honoring my face. The next time I need to find a host for a website, I'll know where to look.

Beyond looking at how to save face for someone else or keep someone from losing face in the first place, it's also just as important for a successful leader at times to look in the mirror. Your concern should be to consider not only how others might lose face, but also whether your own actions could inadvertently cause someone to lose face.

Everyone makes mistakes, and when it happens, the most difficult thing to do is also the best thing you can do—own up to it. Admit your mistake, let them know that your intent was not to hurt them or demean them in any way, and make things right. Setting a good example and making amends is one of the most powerful leadership qualities a true leader can have.

The one final point I'd like everyone to take away from this book is that the idea of saving and honoring face is evident in just about every interaction in our lives, both business and personal. In the last section of this book, "The Toolkit," I've compiled a checklist to help you navigate areas where face is involved. At the very least, I hope the work here provides a lens for anyone to gain a clearer perspective on what motivates and sustains people as it pertains to face.

Face is an attribute imperceptible to most,
but unmistakably apparent to those
who understand its reach.

Now that we've gone through the various aspects of saving face, let's boil it down to the basics.

Remember crib notes or cheat sheets? Some of you may remember your schoolteacher allowing you to fit as much information as possible on a sheet of paper to bring in for a test. The flowchart provided here serves as your own set of crib notes to use when you are dealing with issues of face. It illustrates the three key aspects of what a leader does with issues of face: saving face, honoring face, and providing feedback about face.

Saving Face. There is never a time when you shouldn't be trying to save or protect face. Setting that aside, there are times when it's particularly important to employ strategies to keep others from feeling diminished, humiliated, or devalued.

When a situation or action occurs that could negatively impact a team or individual, be inclusive in your communication and coordination with the group. Promote the idea that you are all working toward common goals and that you all take wins and losses as a team. The key is to turn a situation around to prevent the loss of respect or dignity for all parties involved, in order to reach a positive outcome.

Use the BUILD model (chapter 6):

- Practice **Benevolence and Accountability**—treat others as *they* would like to be treated, but also hold them accountable for their actions and behaviors.

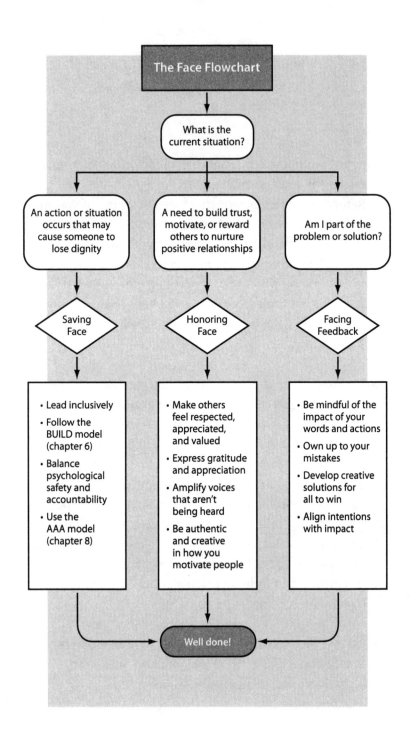

- **Understand** the situation and ask questions so that you are fully informed.

- **Interact** in an inclusive way and invite different perspectives.

- **Learn** all about the issue at hand and the potential solutions available.

- **Deliver** a solution based on your understanding of the available options.

Create an environment where others feel safe and comfortable enough to propose solutions or new ideas. Leave your ego at the door and be aware of others' values and frames of reference.

Think of face as social currency. Build a supply of face with someone by continuously making deposits, just like a bank account. The more we deposit, the more we build trust. If we mistakenly cause someone to lose face, the relationship can still be saved if there are enough deposits to cover the withdrawal.

Honoring Face. Honoring face follows along with the idea of building a supply of face. It happens when you make others feel respected and valued. Express gratitude and appreciation for a job well done and bring in voices from those in the group who aren't heard often enough. Authenticity is the key—you have to mean it.

Be creative in how to honor face. Financial rewards are not the only way to motivate people. Recognition can come in many forms. Surprise people.

When people feel they are valued as part of a team, that is when the team starts to gel and obstacles are overcome.

Being part of the problem or part of the solution. Before looking at everything else to identify a problem or bottleneck, it often helps to take a good look in the mirror. Are you doing everything you can to protect the face of others?

Always be attentive to your words and actions. If you make a mistake, own up to it and accept responsibility. Simply taking responsibility in a genuine way actually leads to a deposit of face into your own account.

Don't always look at an issue as a win/lose proposition. Think creatively. Are there options where everyone can benefit? Think outside of the box and encourage others to share their ideas.

Encourage feedback—learn from what you've done in the past and how your choices have impacted others. As you look to the future, align your best intentions with the impact of your actions. Mean what you say.

No amount of tips can cover every eventuality when it comes to face, but that's not the point. A problem is seldom perfectly settled by a single action you take on a particular day. Rather, it's the totality of the goodwill you've established that will ultimately overcome every situation. This guide is meant to set you on your way.

Good luck!

NOTES

Chapter 1 Saving Face as Social Currency

1. Jeremy Solomons, interview by author, August 26, 2016.
2. Dan Nesselroth, interview by author, March 22, 2019.
3. Yen Tu, interview by author, April 16, 2019.

Chapter 2 How to Avoid Losing Face

1. Brené Brown, *The Gifts of Imperfection: Let Go of Who You Think You're Supposed to Be and Embrace Who You Are* (Center City, Minn.: Hazelden, 2010).
2. Jasmine Garsd, "In an Increasingly Polarized America, Is It Possible to Be Civil on Social Media?," NPR, March 31, 2019, https://www.npr.org/2019/03/31/708039892/in-an-increasingly-polarized-america-is-it-possible-to-be-civil-on-social-media.
3. Hanna Rosin, "The End of Empathy," NPR, April 15, 2019, https://www.npr.org/2019/04/15/712249664/the-end-of-empathy.
4. Eugene Burdick and William J. Lederer, *The Ugly American* (Norton, 1958).
5. Tony Alessandra and Michael J. O'Connor, *The Platinum Rule* (Grand Central Publishing, 2008).
6. Kiyoshi Matsumoto, "Face Is Everything in Japan," Talk About Japan, May 2, 2018, https://talkaboutjapan.com/save-face-in-japanese-culture/.
7. Hannah Hutyra, "114 Bruce Lee Quotes That Will Trigger Personal Growth," https://www.keepinspiring.me/bruce-lee-quotes/.
8. Ibid.
9. Ibid.

Chapter 3 Authentic Acts of Saving and Honoring Face

1. "Have a Nice Day," Wikipedia, https://en.wikipedia.org/wiki/Have_a_nice_day.
2. Brown, *The Gifts of Imperfection*.
3. Pema Chödrön, *The Places That Scare You: A Guide to Fearlessness in Difficult Times* (Boston: Shambhala, 2001).
4. Brown, *The Gifts of Imperfection*.

Chapter 4 Saving Face for the Wrong Reason

1. Kim Scott, "What Steve Jobs Taught Me about Debate in the Workplace," Better, *NBC News*, March 14, 2017, https://www.nbcnews.com/better/careers/what-steve-jobs-taught-me-about-debate-workplace-n732956.
2. Ibid.

Chapter 5 Psychological Safety, Innovation, . . . and Face

1. Amy C. Edmondson and Kathryn S. Roloff, "Leveraging Diversity through Psychological Safety," *Rotman Management Magazine*, September 1, 2009.

2. Charles Duhigg, "What Google Learned from Its Quest to Build the Perfect Team," *The New York Times Magazine*, February 25, 2016, https://www.nytimes.com/2016/02/28/magazine/what-google-learned-from-its-quest-to-build-the-perfect-team.html.

3. Edmondson and Roloff, "Leveraging Diversity through Psychological Safety."

4. Duhigg, "What Google Learned from Its Quest to Build the Perfect Team."

5. Darlene Solomon, interview by author, April 8, 2018.

6. Francesca Gino, "The Business Case for Curiosity," *Harvard Business Review* (September–October 2018), https://hbr.org/2018/09/curiosity#the-business-case-for-curiosity.

Chapter 6 How to BUILD Relationships Using Face

1. N. Nayab, "Three Different Types of Communication: Verbal, Nonverbal & Visual," Bright Hub PM, July 25, 2010, https://www.brighthubpm.com/methods-strategies/79297-comparing-various-forms-of-communication/.

2. Gregory Wallace, "Bill Gates: 'I feel pretty stupid that I don't know any foreign languages,'" CNN Business, January 28, 2015, https://money.cnn.com/2015/01/28/technology/bill-gates-regret/index.html.

3. John Spence, "How to Become an Expert," JohnSpence.com, September 20, 2014, https://blog.johnspence.com/expert/.

4. Malcolm Gladwell, *Outliers: The Story of Success* (New York: Little, Brown, Hachette Book Group, 2008).

5. "The Johari Window Model," Communication Theory, https://www.communicationtheory.org/the-johari-window-model/.

Chapter 8 Cultural Agility

1. Geert Hofstede, "Geert Hofstede's: The Dimension Paradigm," Hofstede Insights, https://www.hofstede-insights.com/models/.

2. Edward T. Hall, *The Silent Language* (New York: Anchor Books, 1973, 1990).

Chapter 9 Seeing beyond the Glass Ceiling

1. Carol S. Dweck, *Mindset: The New Psychology of Success* (New York: Penguin Random House, 2006, 2016).

2. Berit Brogaard, "Micro-Inequities: 40 Years Later," *Psychology Today*, April 20, 2013, https://www.psychologytoday.com/us/blog/the-superhuman-mind/201304/micro-inequities-40-years-later.

Chapter 10 Face and the Value of Feedback

1. Marcus Buckingham and Ashley Goodall, "The Feedback Fallacy," *Harvard Business Review* (March–April 2019), https://hbr.org/2019/03/the-feedback-fallacy.

2. Bill Bundy, interview by author, March 11, 2019.

ACKNOWLEDGMENTS

Wayne, my devastatingly handsome husband—I couldn't have done it without you. You are my best friend, my rock, and the love of my life. Thank you for always being there for me.

Tyler, Savannah, and Ethan, my triplets—Thanks for teaching me about love, patience, and resilience. I love being your mother.

Darlene Solomon, Jeremy Solomons, Patty McKay, Shannon Basile, Bill Bundy, Dan Nesselroth, Ron Lewis, Yen Tu, Prabal Cupta, Rita Wuebbeler, Pam Bundy, Chaoxiong You, and Heather Robinson—Thanks for sharing your fascinating stories and valuable life lessons about saving and honoring face.

Diana K. Rowland—Thanks for your friendship and support all these years. You are my role model for compassion, wisdom, grace, and humility.

Steve Piersanti, my editor—Thanks for believing in me and coaching me throughout the writing process to gain clarity about my core message. You have given me "straight talk" feedback to make the book stronger and better. I have learned so much from you. It was truly a privilege and honor to work with you.

Judith Katz—Thank you for connecting me to Steve Piersanti and Berrett-Koehler Publishers. It was a game changer and I can't thank you enough.

Edward Iwata and Marla Caceres—Thanks for your strong collaboration and believing in the message of this book. You have helped to make this book a reality in a very significant way.

Frances Hesselbein, Frank Wagner, Jim Moore, Bill

Hawkins, and Carlos Marin—Thanks for your generosity, wisdom, and friendship. You have been an inspiration to me all these years. I am lucky to call you my friends.

Marshall Goldsmith—Thank you for being my mentor, my teacher, and my friend for more than thirty years. My life is better off because of you.

Ann Bowers-Evangelista, Brian Underhill, Barbara McMahon, Tom Akins, Val Markos, Beth Schumaker, Carlos Paulet, Carolyn Maue, Simon Vetter, Susan Diamond, Chris Fehrnstrom, Nancy Parsons, Scott Eblin, Greg Zlevor, Patricia Wheeler, Larry Levin, Helfried Albrecht, Jim Intagliata, Lisa Walker, Jodi Knox, Peter Berner, and Rebecca Turner—Thanks to my colleagues in Alexcel Group for your encouragement, generosity, and friendship. I am honored and blessed to be part of this amazing group.

Diane Vere—Thanks for being my coach and asking me the hard questions. You inspired me to discover my purpose and follow my passion.

Joel Garfinkle—Thanks for being my accountability partner. I am so grateful for your support in my journey to get this book done.

Gregg Ward and Cynthia Burnham—Thanks for your encouragement and enthusiasm for this book, and for inviting me to join your amazing Mastermind group. I am honored and humbled.

Judith Eberl, Eun Kim, Rosa Grunhaus Belzer, Robin Speculand, Brigitta Wurnig, CB Bowman, Louis Carter, Mark C. Thompson, Matthias Brose, May Busch, Paul McManus, Meredith Bell, Mike Howard, Neal Goodman, Deborah Grayson Riegel, Denise Pirrotti Hummel, Ken Wheatley, Wendy Tan, and Walter Meyer—Thanks for your endorsement, support, and friendship.

Gitfon Cheung—Thanks for being my sister and my best friend. I am grateful to have you in my life.

And Ally . . . thank you for all the love and happiness.

INDEX

AAA model: for cultural agility, 103–108; millennials, knowledge workers and, 108–111; "no" used with, 111–113
acceptance of feedback, 27
accommodation, 90, 119–120
accountability, 45; with benevolence, 61–63, 157; in BUILD model, 61–66, 82; saving face with, 12
acquiring cultural knowledge, AAA model step and, 105–106
action, 4, 8, 34; culture influencing, 97; internal dialogue guiding, 130–131; others impacted by, 32–33, 123
adapting new behaviors:, AAA model step, and, 105–106; in new situations, 128–129
Agilent Technologies, 55, 115–117
Alessandra, Tony, 25
Alibaba Group, 40–41
alliances, 134–135
ambiguity, 112–113
American culture, Japanese culture and, 111–112
American executives, 3–4, 56–57, 83–86, 108; and BUILD model, 78–81; interacting with Singaporean executive, 71; losing face and Chinese hospitality, 150–151
Americans: behavior of, and losing face, 23–24; coworkers, mentorship and, 106–107; irritating phrases used by, 24–25; stereotype of, 22–23
amplification strategy, 135
appreciation, expressing, 2, 3, 39, 74, 143–145, 158, 159
architect and client, example of, 59–61
Asian culture: and ambiguity, 112–113; Confucianism impacting, 63–64; eye contact within, 91; face represented in, 7–8; negative feedback in, 139; stereotypes of, 25, 36; Western culture compared to, 82
audience, 37; emotional intelligence

for, 35–36; leadership awareness of, 126; self-deprecation influencing, 131
authenticity, 13; face and relationship with, 2–3, 5; saving face with, 31–35
autopilot, executives working on, 87–89

the Beatles, 76
behavior, culture forming, 92
benevolence, 33; accountability with, 61–63, 157; in BUILD model, 61–66, 78, 81, 82, 157; global executive practice of, 65–66, 78, 81, 82
bias, 54–55, 122, 133–134
Bill and Melinda Gates Foundation, 76
blunt talk, 34, 140–141
body language, 20, 72
Branson, Jake, 94–95
Brown, Brené, 19, 32
Buckingham, Marcus, 141–142
BUILD model, 61–78; benevolence and accountability in, 61–66, 78, 81, 82, 157; delivery in, 77–78, 81, 159; examples of using, 78–86; global leadership with, 77–78, 86; interacting in, 71–75, 81, 159; Johari Window and, 83–86; learning in, 75–79, 81, 159; understanding in, 66–71, 81, 159
Bundy, Bill, 148
business, 79–80, 96, 109; cultural agility in, 99–113; empowering women in, 126–128; global complexities in, 149–152; high- and low-context-oriented cultures in, 94–95; and human antenna, 92–93; and multicultural perspectives, 68–71; relationship building in, 60; status and reputation in, 7–8

caring, impact on others of, 32–33
Carnegie Deli, 34
Cast Away, 70

166   Index

A globally recognized speaker, author, and Master Certified Executive Coach, Maya Hu-Chan specializes in global leadership, diversity, inclusion, and cross-cultural management.

Maya partners with organizations to build leadership capabilities to enable profound growth and change, aligned with business and personal goals. Maya's ability to significantly advance the leadership effectiveness of executives has led to more than 70 percent of her coaching clients being promoted during or soon after the coaching engagement. She is also a popular keynote speaker and workshop facilitator.

Maya has been honored by the following organizations:

Ranked Top 8 Global Solutions Thinkers by Thinkers50

World's Top 30 Leadership Gurus by Leadership Guru International

Top 100 Thought Leaders in Management & Leadership by Leadership Excellence

President's Leadership Advisory Council for the World Bank

Achieved "Master Certified Coach" level by the International Coach Federation

Nominee for "Woman of the Year" Award by *San Diego Magazine*

"Leading the Global Workforce Best Practice Award" by Linkage Inc.

Founding member, The Marshall Goldsmith Group

Maya has worked with thousands of leaders from major corporations throughout the Americas, Asia, Australia, and Europe. She co-authored the book *Global Leadership: The Next Generation*, which was chosen by Harvard Business School as part of their Working Knowledge book series. She has lectured at the Brookings Institution, the University of California, San Diego, the University of Chicago, the University of Southern California, and the Tuck School of Business at Dartmouth College.

A frequent contributor to business publications and media, she is a columnist for *INC.com*. Her work has appeared in *BusinessWeek, Harvard Business Online, Bloomberg, OD Practitioner, Leadership Excellence, Thinkers50, American Management Association (AMA), Business Coaching Worldwide, SmartBrief on Leadership, Voice America, Asia Media, The Human Factor Magazine* (India), *AthenaOnline,* and *ATD Management Blog.*

Maya lives in San Diego, California, with her husband, Wayne, their triplets, Tyler, Savannah, and Ethan, and their golden retriever, Molly.

Maya is available as a keynote speaker or as an executive coach. For more information, go to www.mayahuchan.com or email her at mayahuchan@TheGlobalLead.com.

Berrett–Koehler
Publishers

Berrett-Koehler is an independent publisher dedicated to an ambitious mission: *Connecting people and ideas to create a world that works for all.*

Our publications span many formats, including print, digital, audio, and video. We also offer online resources, training, and gatherings. And we will continue expanding our products and services to advance our mission.

We believe that the solutions to the world's problems will come from all of us, working at all levels: in our society, in our organizations, and in our own lives. Our publications and resources offer pathways to creating a more just, equitable, and sustainable society. They help people make their organizations more humane, democratic, diverse, and effective (and we don't think there's any contradiction there). And they guide people in creating positive change in their own lives and aligning their personal practices with their aspirations for a better world.

And we strive to practice what we preach through what we call "The BK Way." At the core of this approach is *stewardship,* a deep sense of responsibility to administer the company for the benefit of all of our stakeholder groups, including authors, customers, employees, investors, service providers, sales partners, and the communities and environment around us. Everything we do is built around stewardship and our other core values of *quality, partnership, inclusion,* and *sustainability.*

This is why Berrett-Koehler is the first book publishing company to be both a B Corporation (a rigorous certification) and a benefit corporation (a for-profit legal status), which together require us to adhere to the highest standards for corporate, social, and environmental performance. And it is why we have instituted many pioneering practices (which you can learn about at www.bkconnection.com), including the Berrett-Koehler Constitution, the Bill of Rights and Responsibilities for BK Authors, and our unique Author Days.

We are grateful to our readers, authors, and other friends who are supporting our mission. We ask you to share with us examples of how BK publications and resources are making a difference in your lives, organizations, and communities at www.bkconnection.com/impact.

Dear reader,

Thank you for picking up this book and welcome to the worldwide BK community! You're joining a special group of people who have come together to create positive change in their lives, organizations, and communities.

What's BK all about?

Our mission is to connect people and ideas to create a world that works for all.

Why? Our communities, organizations, and lives get bogged down by old paradigms of self-interest, exclusion, hierarchy, and privilege. But we believe that can change. That's why we seek the leading experts on these challenges—and share their actionable ideas with you.

A welcome gift

To help you get started, we'd like to offer you a **free copy** of one of our bestselling ebooks:

www.bkconnection.com/welcome

When you claim your **free ebook**, you'll also be subscribed to our blog.

Our freshest insights

Access the best new tools and ideas for leaders at all levels on our blog at ideas.bkconnection.com.

Sincerely,

Your friends at Berrett-Koehler